Tanaka 1587

Japan's Greatest Unknown Samurai Battle

Stephen Turnbull

Helion & Company

Helion & Company Limited
Unit 8 Amherst Business Centre
Budbrooke Road
Warwick
CV34 5WE
England
Tel. 01926 499 619
Email: info@helion.co.uk
Website: www.helion.co.uk
Twitter: @helionbooks
Visit our blog at http://blog.helion.co.uk/

Published by Helion & Company 2019
Designed and typeset by Mach 3 Solutions Ltd (www.mach3solutions.co.uk)
Cover designed by Paul Hewitt, Battlefield Design (www.battlefield-design.co.uk)
Printed by Henry Ling Limited, Dorchester

ISBN 978-1-912866-49-6

British Library Cataloguing-in-Publication Data.
A catalogue record for this book is available from the British Library.

For details of other military history titles published by Helion & Company Limited, contact the above address, or visit our website: http://www.helion.co.uk

We always welcome receiving book proposals from prospective authors.

Contents

Author's Note

Japanese names are given in the conventional style of family name/clan name first, personal name second, e.g. Toyotomi Hideyoshi not Hideyoshi Toyotomi. Note, however, that the personal name is normally used as the identifier in a textual narrative. So, for example, 'Hideyoshi ordered an attack', not 'Toyotomi ordered an attack'.

The portrait of Mōri Hidekane used here is owned by the Gensaiji temple in Yamaguchi Prefecture. It is reproduced here by kind permission of the Chief Priest and was supplied by Yamaguchi City Board of Education Cultural Properties Protection Division. All the other photographs used in this book were taken by the author and are distributed through his own 'Japan Archive' Picture Library (www.stephenturnbull.com).

This book is dedicated to Audrey Pepper, with much affection.

Foreword

By Jonathan Clements

Historians improve with age, like fine wines. Our libraries expand; our contact lists flourish; we start to get a sense for when a new book idea is taking shape in our footnotes. In the forty years since he wrote *Samurai Armies*, Stephen Turnbull has not lost the infectious, giddy sense of excitement he manages to impart whenever he pokes around a meadow, squinting into the tree-line and gurning at the weather. Ten years ago, in my *Brief History of the Samurai*, I noted that:

> Unlike many armchair historians, Turnbull has trudged over many of the battlefields himself, step by thoughtful step, often producing unexpected and trenchant speculations that are no less worthy than the textual analyses of old chronicles...

He would be the first to admit that he has added to this skillset with newer abilities acquired in academia. You need only compare his *Ninja* (1991) with his *Ninja: Unmasking the Myth* (2018) to see that Turnbull is constantly in competition with himself, seeking new proofs and evidence, challenging his own conclusions in search of a better grand narrative. You can learn, as did he, about historical method and Japanese textual analysis. But they don't teach you to stand in a field and pace out the likely direction of a cavalry charge from 400 years ago. There's no telling what you'll discover on the site, but Turnbull's the kind of historian who will literally walk that extra mile, just in case.

Inspired by his example, I undertook a quest of my own around Kyushu, tracking the progress of the Shimabara Rebellion of 1637–8. Modern Japan might well be a jumble of storm drains and concrete jetties, but physical interaction with the places I was writing about soon paid rich dividends. Local museum curators threw open their doors and pressed priceless materials into my hands. My own eyes told me things that ancient sagas neglected to mention, about the distance to the next island or the likelihood that a scout could see from the mountain-top. And interactions with locals provided deep insights into the lasting impact of a forgotten samurai war, in everything from shifts in regional slang to oddities in local delicacies.

It's all that Stephen Turnbull's fault, I observed to the incumbent Mrs Clements, as she retched her way through an authentic Shimabara dish of marine offal – an experience which generated an entire page about siege cuisine in the eventual book. But I also fell in love with the tall green hills and glittering bays of Kyushu, and the atavistic legends that shimmered in its folklore, often leaping out at me from Japanese documents or asides by museum guides, as my eyes refused to believe what they saw. Seriously? A samurai warlord clad in a bearskin, mistaken by enemy troops for a shapeshifting animal? Christian barons leading pogroms against Buddhist temples? Jezebel, the infamous witch-queen of Ōtomo? Portuguese missionaries convincing everybody to try sponge cake...?

In this, his eightieth book, Turnbull demonstrates that there is still so much more to say about Japanese history. As he explains, the story of the siege of Tanaka has only really come to light in the last few decades, as an agglomeration of old chronicles, modern archaeology and a wide-ranging local museum outreach programme. If you are reading this, Tanaka now has a footprint in the English language – a handy introduction for both travellers and historians, loaded with original research and primary source material. And Turnbull does not disappoint in his appending of yet more spectacular imagery to the verifiable historical record – a river running red with blood, a warrior "more bear than man," and a Beatles connection I will leave you to find out for yourself.

Jonathan Clements's publications include *Christ's Samurai: The True Story of the Shimabara Rebellion* and *A Brief History of Japan*. He has presented several seasons of *Route Awakening*, a TV series on Chinese historical icons, for National Geographic Asia.

Timeline

1550		The Wani family declare their support for Kikuchi Yoshitake
1578		Battle of Mimigawa and defeat of the Ōtomo
1579		The Ryuzoji invade Higo; the Wani join in the battle of Shiratori
1581		The Shimazu invade southern Higo and besiege Minamata
1584		Ryuzoki Takanobu dies at Okita-Nawate; the Shimazu invade Higo
1586		Siege of Iwaya Castle and the battle of Hetsugigawa
Tenshō 15	**8 February 1587 – 27 January 1588**	
3m 1d	8 April	Hideyoshi leaves Osaka for the Kyushu campaign
3m 28d	5 May	Hideyoshi arrives at Kokura Castle
4m 12d	19 May	Hideyoshi meets the Higo barons at Nankan
5m 8d	13 June	Shimazu Yoshihisa surrenders to Hideyoshi
6m 2d	7 July	Sassa Narimasa is appointed to the fief of northern Higo
6m 6d	11 July	Sassa Narimasa enters Kumamoto Castle
7m 1d	4 August	Sassa Narimasa orders a land survey of Higo
7m 23d	26 August	Kobayakawa Takakage informs Hideyoshi about the Higo Rebellion
7m 24d	27 August	Sassa Narimasa sends an army against Waifu Castle
7m 27d	30 August	Fall of Waifu Castle
8m 6d	9 September	Hideyoshi appoints Kobayakawa Takakage as Commander-in-Chief
8m 7d	10 September	The siege of Jōmura Castle begins
8m 8d	11 September	Sassa Narimasa orders the building of two support castles
8m 12d	15 September	A rebel attack on Kumamoto Castle begins
8m 13d	16 September	Sassa's attack on Jōmura is repulsed
8m 14d	17 September	Sassa's nephew Muneyoshi is ambushed and killed at Ueki
8m 15d	18 September	Sassa arrives in Kumamoto Castle and the rebels withdraw
8m 17d	20 September	Sassa Narimasa returns to Jōmura Castle
9m 7d	8 October	Rebels attack the supply column and the Wani fortify Tanaka Castle

9m 8d	9 October	Letter from Hideyoshi setting out reinforcement options
9m 15d	16 October	Letter from Hideyoshi confirming the strategy
9m 19d	20 October	Letter from Hideyoshi referring to Ankokuji Ekei
10m 1d	1 November	Grand Kitano Tea Ceremony
10m 6d	6 November	Kobayakawa Takakage reports to Hideyoshi
10m 16d	25 November	The besieging army arrives at Tanaka
10m 22d	22 November	Letter from Hideyoshi refers to Tanaka Castle being fortified
10 (end)		Uchikoga Shigefusa shuts himself up in Shimono Castle
11m 2d	1 December	First attack on Tanaka Castle
12m 5d	3 January	Fall of Tanaka Castle
12m 6d	4 January	Alternative date for fall of Tanaka Castle
12m 10d	8 January	Letter from Hideyoshi to Kobayakawa notes the palisade
12m 13d	11 January	Sassa's general attacks the Uchikoga in Shimono Castle
12m 15d	13 January	Sassa writes a letter describing the 'clean sweep' of Tanaka
12m 17d	15 January	Kobayakawa reports that Jōmura Castle has surrendered
12m 27d	25 January	The Uchikoga abandon Shimono Castle
Tenshō 16	**28 January 1588–14 February 1589**	
1m	Jan/Feb	Hideyoshi orders Ōtomo Yoshimune to attack Shimonojō Tsunetaka
1m 20d	16 February	Hideyoshi sends the Jōshi-shū into Higo
2m 5d	13 March	Shimazu Yoshihiro enters Higo but is stopped by the Sagara
3m 3d	29 March	Uchikoga Shigefusa is killed attacking Yanagawa Castle
4m	April	The land survey of Higo is completed
4m 3d	18 April	Sassa Narimasa is detained at the Hōonji in Amagasaki
4m 8d	23 April	Murder of Ōtsuyama Iekado
4m 16d	1 May	Nawa Akiteru is killed after leaving Uto Castle
5m 25d	18 June	Kitazato Masayoshi is given the Shimonojō fief
	24 June	The intercalary fifth month begins)
5m 14d (Int)	7 July	Sassa Narimasa commits suicide at the Hōonji
6m 7d	30 July	Letter from Katō reports the destruction of the Shimonojō heirs
6m 13d	5 August	Katō and Konishi are granted Higo Province between them
6m 27d	19 August	Katō and Konishi take over their new castles of Kumamoto and Uto.
8m 8d	28 September	Proclamation of the Sword Hunt
9m 20d	8 November	Death of the last Higo rebel Uchikoga Shigeteru at Makino Castle

Tenshō 17:   **15 February 1589–4 February 1590**

The Amakusa Rebellion

8m 1d	10 September	Konishi demands corvée labour from the Amakusa barons
9m 22d	31 October	Konishi sends an army against Shiki Rinsen
9m 25d	3 November	Konishi's army is defeated at Shiki Castle
11m 3d	10 December	Siege of Shiki Castle begins
11m 10d	17 December	Siege of Hondo begins
11m 25d	1 January	Fall of Hondo Castle
11m 28d	4 January	Katō Kiyomasa withdraws to Kumamoto
1592		The Umekita Rebellion breaks out
1593		Suicide of Aso Koreteru

The bullet holes in this helmet on display in Karatsu Castle show the devastating effects of musket fire.

1

The Unearthing of Tanaka Castle

In 1587 the 1,000-strong garrison of tiny Tanaka Castle in Higo Province (modern Kumamoto Prefecture) on Japan's southern island of Kyushu, held out for one hundred days against an army ten times their size sent by the great general Toyotomi Hideyoshi. When the castle fell it was burned to the ground, and for four centuries the epic struggle lived on only through a handful of letters, two little-known war chronicles and in the folk memories of the local people who continued to make offerings to the tormented spirits of Tanaka's dead warriors.

In 1986 everything changed. Prompted by the approaching fourth centenary of the battle the local council set in motion a systematic archaeological investigation of the castle site. Many interesting finds were made, but the greatest discovery of all came in 1989 in a distant library where a researcher unearthed what turned out to be Japan's oldest surviving battle map. It featured a detailed drawing of Tanaka Castle during the siege that matched up exactly to the picture that was emerging from the excavation. The unique document also contained so much extra information that, when combined with the archaeological finds, the written materials and local folklore, the almost forgotten siege of Tanaka became one of the best documented battles in the whole of Japanese history. This book will tell the complete story of that epic struggle for the first time.

Toyotomi Hideyoshi (1536–98) was one of the most important figures in Japanese history. He rose through the ranks of Oda Nobunaga's army to command provinces and ultimately the whole of Japan. His invasion of Kyushu was the largest military campaign on Japanese soil to that date. He also set in motion several far-reaching reforms involving land reform, the separation of the military and farming classes and the disarmament of the latter.

My personal discovery of the siege of Tanaka began in 2009 in Kumamoto Prefectural Library, where I came across a book about the Higo Rebellion: the local uprising against Hideyoshi within which the Tanaka battle was a small but significant episode. My interest then was in a later revolt within Higo that took place on the Amakusa Islands in 1589, but the wealth of little known source material for the Tanaka campaign promised a much richer historical experience.[1] This was confirmed when I visited the site in 2010 and was immediately struck by its fine state of preservation and the strong local interest in Tanaka's proud history. I returned to study the castle and the surrounding area six times over the next eight years, and also had the pleasure of twice witnessing its annual festival, of which the climax is a noisy, enthusiastic and highly inaccurate recreation of the battle.

Sources for the Siege of Tanaka

The defence of Tanaka Castle against overwhelming odds was an important part of the Higo Rebellion, but until recently it has remained little-known within Japan and almost completely unknown outside it, with no specific account of the Tanaka action being included in any book-length study until Araki Eishi wrote *Higo Kunishū Ikki* (The Higo Rebellion) in 1987.[2] The work is a thorough study of the overall progress of the Higo Rebellion, although his 12-page account of the Tanaka campaign was drawn only from the literary sources because the archaeological investigation had not yet begun. *Higo Kunishū Ikki* was extensively revised and republished with updated material in 2012.[3]

In 1993 local historian Kunitake Yoshiteru produced *Tenshō Jidai to Wani ichizoku: Higo Kunishū Ikki* (The Wani family of the Tenshō Era and the Higo Rebellion), the first full-length book to deal specifically with the Tanaka operation. It benefited from the archaeological excavations and the battle map, and also drew upon the results of academic discussions about the archaeological discoveries.[4] Ten years later Oyama Ryūshu published *Hideyoshi to Higo Kunishū Ikki* (Hideyoshi and the Higo Rebellion). Its 40-page section on Tanaka is more extensive than Araki's, and it too draws upon the battle map and the archaeology reports.[5]

All three of these books make use of the oldest primary source materials available for the Higo Rebellion, which are the letters exchanged between Toyotomi Hideyoshi and the generals who were campaigning in Kyushu on his behalf. The other written sources for the Tanaka campaign are two lively accounts compiled about 70 years after the event, both of which remained in

---

1   For a full account of the later campaign see: Turnbull, Stephen 2013 'The ghosts of Amakusa: localised opposition to centralised control in Higo Province, 1589–90.' *Japan Forum* 25 (2) 2013, pp. 191–211.
2   Araki Eishi, 1987. *Higo Kunishū Ikki.* Kumamoto: Shuppan Bunka Kaikan.
3   Araki Eishi, 2012. *Higo Kunishū Ikki.* Kumamoto: Shuppan Bunka Kaikan.
4   Kunitake Yoshiteru, 1993. *Tenshō Jidai to Wani ichizoku: Higo Kunishū Ikki.* Kumamoto: Kumamoto Hibi Shimbun Jōhō Bunka Centre.
5   Oyama Ryūshu, 2003. *Hideyoshi to Higo Kunishū Ikki.* Fukuoka: Kaichōsha.

manuscript form until 2000 when they were included in a compendium of historical documents relating to Kumamoto Prefecture.[6] The first is entitled *Wani Gundan* (the Wani war story). It is not dated but a reference to Wani Chikazane's son, who was born shortly after the battle, being still alive at the time of writing would suggest a date of about 1650 at the latest.[7] Although *Wani Gundan* contains many romantic elements in the style of a medieval *gunkimono* ('war tale') several points of detail concerning troop layouts have been confirmed by the discovery of the battle map, suggesting that *Wani Gundan* is largely reliable and that its author probably drew upon family records and oral tradition from participants in the battle or from their descendants. In 2010 a local scholar called Miyao Yoichi republished the text of *Wani Gundan* alongside a paraphrase in modern Japanese.[8]

The second document is a very brief account of the Tanaka campaign entitled *Wani no jō rakujō no oboe* (Memories of the fall of Wani castle). Its authorship is credited to a lay priest called Nakamura Jōshin Nyūdō, who is likely to have been the son of one of the participants.[9] The siege is also mentioned in various contemporary manuscripts relating to the area and in later historical works such as *Higo Kokushi* of 1706, while a wealth of local folklore about the battle has also long existed and includes the enshrinement of certain tragic victims of the conflict as guardian *kami* (deities). This has kept the memory of the siege alive among the local people, who have maintained the graves and shrines around the castle site for over four centuries.

In recent years these source materials have been greatly augmented by the thorough archaeological investigation of the well-preserved site of the castle between 1986 and 2002 and the fortuitous discovery of the map. Detailed reports have been produced and discussed at a series of meetings and symposia, and an annual bulletin about the dig was published until 2002 when the archaeological investigation was completed and the site was conserved. Reports and articles have continued to appear since 1998 via a modest yet scholarly newsletter and through the local press.

The discovery of the battle map in 1989 attracted wide publicity for Tanaka, and in 2002 its story inspired a feature film by director Miike Takashi. His movie *Kumamoto Monogatari* consists of three short stories, the third of which is the siege of Tanaka presented as a highly fictionalised melodrama. It was shot partly on location at the castle site, where local pride has ensured that the hill of Tanaka has been preserved as a small-scale tourist attraction that is easily accessible with good paths and excellent signage. Statues of the three Wani brothers who defended it to the death now greet the visitor at the exit of the car park.

During my 2013 and 2016 visits to Tanaka I was accompanied by Kuroda Yūji, the then Chairman of the Nagomi Town Board of Education. I would particularly like to thank Yūji and his colleagues, all of whom have been very

6   Kumamoto City, 2000. *Kumamoto-shi shi kankei shiryōshū. Volume 4: Higo koki shūran.* Kumamoto: Kumamoto City, pp. 63–66.
7   Kumamoto 2000, p. 66.
8   Miyao Yoichi, ed., 2010. *Nankan Kibun.* Nankan City: Nankan Board of Education., pp. 42–49.
9   Kumamoto 2000, p. 431.

helpful and cooperative in explaining the significance of minor details of the castle site, showing me artefacts and helping me read local place names. My translation of the two key historical documents was greatly advanced following my meeting with Miyao Yoichi in Nankan City in 2013. Above all I wish to thank local historian Maehara Daisaku who pointed me in many fruitful directions and was such good company on several visits to Tanaka.

Thanks to their cooperation I am able to offer the following as a systematic and detailed exercise in micro-history, whereby an in-depth analysis of a local event illuminates the wider national picture. To do this I shall compare and critically combine the evidence concerning Tanaka that is available from history, literature, folklore and archaeology. Before 1987 the siege of Tanaka Castle was virtually unknown beyond its immediate boundaries. Thirty years of painstaking work and enthusiastic publicity have transformed its status within Japan, so I hope that this book will enable Tanaka's story to be understood and appreciated by a much wider international audience.

Stephen Turnbull

2

The Floating Warriors

The siege of Tanaka Castle took place during the Higo Kunishū Ikki (The Higo Rebellion), an uprising that occurred within Higo Province from 1587 to 1588 against an unpopular overlord imposed upon the local population by the future ruler of Japan: Toyotomi Hideyoshi (1536–98). The Higo Rebellion broke out shortly after Hideyoshi's conquest of Kyushu: the largest military campaign ever conducted on Japanese soil and a vital step towards the reunification of Japan, a feat Hideyoshi was to achieve in 1591. His triumph would prove to be a major event in Japanese history, but to understand why reunification should have been either necessary or desirable we have to backtrack a few centuries.

Japan's Age of Warring States

In the year 1185 the Minamoto family had been victorious in the Gempei War, a conflict that had pitted two military families against each other for the first time in Japanese history. The Gempei War led to the reduction of imperial power and the establishment of a permanent form of the once temporary position of shogun, who proceeded to rule Japan as a military dictator. Government by a shogun suffered several mishaps over the following centuries, and the most serious setback was the Ōnin War of 1467–77. That tragic conflict began when a succession dispute within the shogun's own family of Ashikaga led to fighting in Kyoto, Japan's capital. Much of Kyoto was devastated, and when the conflict spread to the provinces the shogun seemed powerless to stop it. The Ōnin War became the start of the century-long Sengoku Period (The Age of Warring States), where we first read of rival warlords commonly called *sengoku daimyō* (great names of the warring states) fighting each other in a bewildering succession of civil wars and rebellions.

Japan may still have been nominally united under the shogun by the grace of the sacred emperor, a man who possessed even less political power than the shogun, but in practical terms no one seemed able to control the *sengoku daimyō*. Naturally enough, the strongest among them dreamed of achieving the reunification of Japan under their own rule by taking control of the shogunate,

A map of Higo Province (modern Kumamoto Prefecture) showing the main places and families associated with the Higo Rebellion of 1587. Castles are shown in lower case. The areas controlled by the kokujin are indicated by their names in capitals.

which was still an institution that commanded unusual respect in spite of its military ineffectiveness. For example, in 1559 the incumbent shogun would give the official title of *shugo* (shogun's deputy) of Owari Province to an up-and-coming local warlord called Oda Nobunaga (1534–82). The honour meant little in military terms to Nobunaga; its value lay instead in giving him official approval for his complete takeover of the province. Over the course of the next decade Oda Nobunaga defeated all his local rivals in battle. He proved to be an innovative military genius, but Nobunaga was also fortunate because fate had placed him quite close to Kyoto. Other more powerful rivals had been prevented from marching on the capital by geography alone, but in 1568 Nobunaga entered the city in triumph and set up his own nominee as the fifteenth and (as it turned out) last shogun of the ill-fated Ashikaga dynasty.

Nobunaga's takeover of the shogunate marked the start of Japan's reunification, which would take a further quarter of a century to complete. It was largely a military operation that would be enforced by land surveys, the transfer of landowners and forcible disarmament. The final result would be a shift from the rule by self-determined *sengoku daimyō* to a national hegemony where the re-defined *daimyō* were men appointed by the national ruler out of the ranks of his most loyal generals. Yet that national ruler was not to be Oda Nobunaga, because he died in 1582 after a military coup. He had been resting in Kyoto, making ready to move west to join a campaign against the Mōri family. Realising that Nobunaga was unusually isolated and weakly defended, a treacherous general launched a surprise attack on him. Thoroughly overwhelmed, Nobunaga committed suicide.

Order was restored to the capital within days of Nobunaga's death by his loyal – albeit opportunistic – general Toyotomi Hideyoshi. Hideyoshi hastily patched up a peace settlement with the Mōri and rushed back to Kyoto, where he defeated the usurper at the battle of Yamazaki. The situation soon developed into a Hideyoshi takeover of Japan, and in a series of battles Hideyoshi defeated his rivals and carried on with the programme of reunification where Nobunaga had left off. Because he had risen through the ranks owing to his military talent Hideyoshi inspired a deep sense of loyalty among his followers, whose numbers would swell whenever Hideyoshi's might was displayed, as it would be in no uncertain fashion against the rebels of Higo Province between 1587 and 1588.

The crushing of the Higo Rebellion is the underlying theme of this book, but it may help the reader if we first take the story on a few years, because Hideyoshi's loyal generals went on to assist him in the conquest of the whole of Japan, with the last independent *sengoku daimyō* capitulating peacefully in 1591. Unfortunately for Japan, Hideyoshi then over-reached himself by mounting an invasion of Korea in 1592. The disastrous expedition seriously weakened his supporters, and when Hideyoshi died in 1598 leaving an infant son as his heir chaos threatened to return. The former generals of Hideyoshi split into two warring factions: those who supported young Toyotomi Hideyori, and those who believed he was less capable of ruling Japan than they were. Matters were resolved by the victory of Tokugawa Ieyasu (1542–1616) at the battle of Sekigahara in 1600. He was proclaimed shogun in 1603. The 'rightful king' Toyotomi Hideyori perished during the siege of Osaka Castle in 1615, leaving the Tokugawa family free to rule Japan, which they did until 1868. Their era was called the Tokugawa or Edo Period from the name of the new shogun's capital of Edo, the city which we now know as Tokyo.

Higo Province and the *Sengoku Daimyō*

Japan's bloody and often tortuous transition from the wars of the Sengoku Period to its reunification and the peaceful centuries of the Tokugawa Era would mark the passing of Medieval Japan and the beginning of its Early Modern era. In political terms the former had been characterised by the existence of small landownings controlled by petty lords of various shapes and sizes, the strongest and wealthiest of whom were the *sengoku daimyō*. A *sengoku daimyō* ruled his own *kokka*国家(domain), usefully described as 'a political unit defined by the reach of his military and public authority', a phrase that reveals how much of their success depended upon military victories.[1] A *kokka* was no respecter of provincial boundaries and might well possess an untidy geographical shape, consisting as it did of a composite of separate fiefs either held directly by the ruler's family or indirectly by his *kerai* 家来, his closest followers for whom the European term 'retainer' is customarily employed. A *kerai* was bound to his lord by an oath of vassalage. When the process took place as a result of a military victory the defeated leader would pay homage to the victor and accept a subordinate status, following which his lands would be returned to him under an arrangement similar to that of European feudalism.

The model that would characterise Early Modern Japan involved a shift towards centralisation and vassalage under a much smaller number of very powerful provincial lords to whom the single term *daimyō* is invariably applied. These powerful local lords sought to become the absolute masters of their own territories, separating samurai from any involvement in cultivation and reducing all farmers to unarmed tax-paying workers inside a rigid social structure. The system would be set in stone by the Tokugawa family from 1603 onwards, by which time all the surviving *daimyō* had become the shogun's vassals. From then on *daimyō* numbers were strictly controlled and regulated, and they all fully understood that they governed their domains only by delegation from Edo.

During the early 1580s all this strictness and rigidity lay in the future as far as Higo was concerned, although the province already consisted of two different areas that reflected both Japan's future and its past. Much of southern Higo was the domain of the Sagara family, who ruled from their castle of Hitoyoshi, just as their ancestors had done as the shogun's deputies since at least the thirteenth century. During the Sengoku Period the Sagara had made the transition from shogun's appointees to independent *sengoku daimyō,* and under the Tokugawa regime their descendants would rule Kuma District in the south-east of Higo as the *daimyō* of the Hitoyoshi domain. The Sagara were therefore destined to be Higo Province's great survivors, although in 1580 the current lord Sagara Yoshiaki (1544–81) was in a very delicate position, because his southern border impinged most uncomfortably against the lands of the ancient, powerful and extremely belligerent Shimazu family of Satsuma Province (modern Kagoshima Prefecture).

Together with the Ryūzōji of Hizen Province (modern Nagasaki Prefecture) to the north-west and the Ōtomo of Bungo Province (modern Ōita Prefecture) to the north-east, the Shimazu made up Kyushu's 'big three' *sengoku daimyō,* who either fought each other or cemented temporary alliances over a period of several decades.[2] The Shimazu ultimately proved to

---

1 Birt, Michael Patrick, *Warring States: A study of the Go-Hōjō daimyo and domain 1491–1590* (Ph.D Thesis, Princeton University, 1983), p. 47.
2 Araki 1987, p. 15.

Shimazu Yoshihisa (1533–1611) was the head of the independent-minded and highly aggressive Shimazu family of Satsuma. By 1587 the Shimazu had taken over almost all of Kyushu including Higo Province, but were to face the overwhelming force of Hideyoshi's invasion.

be the most successful, and by the late 1570s they had added neighbouring Ōsumi Province (now part of Kagoshima) and much of Hyūga Province (modern Miyazaki Prefecture) to their domains, making them masters of all of southern Kyushu below Higo Province.

Higo would suffer the impact of the armies of the Ōtomo, Ryūzōji and Shimazu in remorseless succession over many years. The Ōtomo, whose early influence will be discussed later, were displaced from the province after being heavily defeated by the Shimazu at the battle of Mimigawa in 1578. Their severe reversal left the Shimazu free to expand into Higo. The coastal route through the province was a vital channel of communication, so

謹賀

Ryuzoji Takanobu was one of the 'big three' daimyō of Kyushu and exerted considerable influence over Higo Province until his death at the hands of his rivals the Shimazu in 1584.

in 1581 the Shimazu took steps to deprive Sagara Yoshiaki of his strategic fortress of Minamata to provide a base for their northward expansion. When Minamata surrendered Yoshiaki's more northerly coastal castles of Sashiki and Yatsushiro fell along with it, reducing the Sagara domain to Kuma District and placing the Shimazu in control of the rest of southern Higo.

Three years later in 1584 the Shimazu exploited their new acquisitions in Higo by crossing the sea from Yatsushiro to Hizen Province, where they inflicted a crushing defeat on the Ryūzōji. The campaign ended with the defeat and death of the *daimyō* Ryūzōji Takanobu (1530–84) at the battle of Okita-Nawate and the extension of Shimazu influence into Hizen. It also opened up northern Higo to the Shimazu for operations against the Ōtomo's remaining domains, and in 1586 the coast road took one division of the Shimazu to victory over the Ōtomo's retainer Takahashi Jōun (1550–86) at Iwaya Castle in Chikuzen Province (modern Fukuoka Prefecture). Meanwhile another Shimazu army veered inland from Yatsushiro and crossed Higo beneath the southern rim of the massive caldera of Mount Aso. Ōtomo's castle of Oka, which guarded the western border of Bungo Province, was then attacked. The success of these operations meant that by the beginning of 1587 the only external influence that counted for anything in Higo Province was that exerted by the Shimazu of Satsuma.

The Barons of Higo

Unlike the position enjoyed for centuries by the Sagara family, throughout this time of conflict there had been no one in the northern part of Higo Province who could be identified as its *sengoku daimyō*. Instead the medieval model of local governance still lived on among the province's forested valleys and high mountain peaks as a patchwork of small landownings held by a number of defiant and manipulative *kokujin* 国人. The word translates simply as 'men of the province', but its significance can vary enormously in contemporary documents. Sometimes it indicates a man at the highest level of the provincial hierarchy who owns a castle, such as the Wani family of Tanaka; alternatively the term can just mean a small landowner whose jurisdiction is limited to one village, thus making him little more than a village headman. John Whitney Hall defines *kokujin* as 'local military proprietors who had the potential to become *daimyō*, or at least high-ranking members of a *kashindan* (a *daimyō*'s retainer band)'. Their followers fought in units called *kunishū* 国衆, defined by Hall as 'organised bands of local warriors who possessed certain superior rights over some land and its workers'.[3] In an article of 1880 J.H. Gubbins called the *kokujin* of Higo 'sworded gentry', while a modern historian has distinguished the more powerful castle-owning *kokujin* from the richer *sengoku daimyō* by using a useful analogy from medieval Europe and calling them 'barons'.[4]

In behavioural terms, however, the distinction was purely a matter of scale, because the barons of Higo behaved exactly like *sengoku daimyō* in many ways, particularly through their willingness to fight each other. The big difference between them lay in their personal wealth, because a typical *kokujin* enjoyed a very modest income compared to a *sengoku daimyō*. For example, in 1587 the Wani barons of Tanaka Castle owned lands worth 2,015 *koku,* while the Sagara family's possessions were assessed as 22,000 *koku*.[5] It is therefore likely that only the senior *bushi* 武士 (warriors, literally 'military gentlemen') in any baron's army could possibly have enjoyed the luxury of being full-time fighting men, a status dependent upon wealth and rank for which the familiar word *samurai* 侍 is normally used. Instead they led armies that consisted largely of *jizamurai* 地侍 (country samurai), a term that indicates their overall status as part-time warriors and farmers.

Because of this dual role the higher ranks in Japanese society did not regard *jizamurai* as full members of the aristocratic samurai class, and it is indeed true that most of them would not have enjoyed anything like the élitism commonly attributed to the name. The familiar image of the samurai as a sword-bearing military aristocrat who never got his hands dirty in a paddy field derives largely from the social stratification of the Tokugawa Period, which would be a time when samurai and farmers were two separate social classes divided by an unbridgeable gulf, with only the former enjoying the exclusive right to wear swords. In 1580, if contemporary writings are to be believed, everyone with something to defend – landowners, villagers, priests and pirates – was armed to the teeth. It was therefore perfectly normal to be both a farmer and a fighter at the same time, and the disordered nature of the times also made it possible to rise within society because of one's talent instead of one's birth. The classic example of this social mobility was of course Toyotomi Hideyoshi himself. His father had been a *jizamurai* in Oda Nobunaga's forces, while Hideyoshi rose to lead armies and then the entire country.

Two documents relating to the Higo Rebellion use a unique and enigmatic expression to identify a particular local brand of fighting men. The word is *ukimusha* 浮武者 (floating warriors). In other contemporary contexts the term *ukimusha* is only encountered as the homophone 遊武者, which

---

3   Hall, John Whitney (ed.), *Japan Before Tokugawa: Political Consolidation and Economic Growth, 1500 to 1650* (Princeton: Princeton University Press, 1981), p. 24 & 208.

4   Gubbins, J.H. 1880. 'Hideyoshi and the Satsuma Clan in the Sixteenth Century' *Transactions of the Asiatic Society of Japan* 8, p. 118; Elisonas, Jurgis, 'Christianity and the daimyo' In Hall, J.W. & McLain, J.L. (eds.), *The Cambridge History of Japan. Vol. 4 Early modern Japan* (Cambridge: Cambridge University Press, 1991), p. 365.

5   Kunitake 1993, p. 115. One *koku* was notionally regarded as the amount of rice needed to feed one man for one year, and during the Sengoku Period was equivalent to approximately 180 litres. Area measurement was another way of expressing wealth and was made in multiples of *chō* (about 1 hectare).

The Kikuchi Shrine in Kikuchi City is built upon the site of Waifu Castle where the Higo Rebellion began. This striking life-sized dummy samurai is on display in the shrine's treasure house, and even though the costume is supposed to depict a samurai of the fourteenth century, his faded, old-fashioned armour and defiant expression perfectly illustrated the lower-class *jizamurai* of the Higo Rebellion. These men were the *ukimusha* (floating warriors) who took on Hideyoshi's army.

military dictionaries define as a reserve corps or flying column of troops who could be moved into action quickly. In *Wani Gundan* the *ukimusha* serve as a separate unit inside Tanaka Castle under their own captain and their ranks include men of retainer status, so Miyao interprets the meaning of *ukimusha* at Tanaka as being the usual one of reserves.[6] In the muster roll for the siege of Jōmura Castle however, the Higo *ukimusha* appear to be distinguished from both samurai and civilians, implying that they formed an intermediate class synonymous with *jizamurai* because they 'floated' between the two roles of samurai and farmers.[7]

There is however an alternative way of looking at the concept of a 'floating warrior' that is very useful in the current narrative, and this concerns the allegiance professed by the *ukimusha*'s masters the *kokujin* of Higo, who 'floated' in a very different way. Throughout the Sengoku Period the Higo barons lived an independent if somewhat precarious existence squeezed in between the three great powers of Kyushu, who had already spent much time and effort taking over very similar *jizamurai* territories within their own home provinces. The Higo *kokujin* therefore had to perform an awkward balancing act between accepting a place in a feudal organisation and staying aloof from it, a choice for which they were helped by the ebb and flow of external

---

6   Miyao 2010, p. 43.
7   Mikawa 1997, pp. 210–211.

influence over Higo, an ever-changing situation that made it possible for them to play off one potential predator against another. Cooperation, expressed usually by accepting vassal status, could be as useful as confrontation for staying afloat on the waves that surged into their province, so over a period of several decades the *kokujin* fought for and against armies marching under the Shimazu, Ōtomo and Ryūzōji banners in a confusing series of alliances and campaigns that somehow managed to avoid, or at the very least delay, their personal extinction. In one extreme and tragic example the *kokujin* family of Akahoshi supplied three children to the Shimazu to be presented as hostages to the Ryūzōji as a pledge of non-aggression. When the Shimazu moved against the Ryūzōji in 1584 one of the children was crucified, so the Akahoshi's feudal obligation to join the Shimazu expedition against Hizen was enhanced by their desire for revenge.[8]

The Ōtomo Family and Higo Province

The much-cherished yet very precarious independence enjoyed by the Higo barons during the 1580s arose largely from how they had been treated by their first overlords the Ōtomo family of Bungo. Reference was made earlier to the military disasters suffered by the Ōtomo and Ryūzōji at the hands of the Shimazu in 1578 and 1584 respectively. Before those dates the Ōtomo of Bungo had been the dominant external force in Higo Province, influencing it under two successive *daimyō*: Ōtomo Yoshiaki (1502–50) and his son Yoshishige, known better to history as Ōtomo Sōrin (1530–87).

The Ōtomo family had been the shogun's deputies of Bungo for centuries. When the Sengoku Period got under way various conflicts gave them control over much of Higo and its *kokujin*, a situation that Yoshiaki formalised in a highly symbolic manner in 1520 when he installed his young teenage brother as the fictitious heir of Higo's extinct Kikuchi family. Kikuchi Yoshitake, as he was now called, became *shugo* of Higo, so the *kokujin* were able to show their loyalty to the Ōtomo by following a lord who was supposedly one of their own. However, it proved to be Yoshitake himself who questioned the notion of loyalty to the Ōtomo, because on achieving maturity he took a very independent line and rebelled against his brother in 1550.

In that same year Ōtomo Yoshiaki was murdered in a palace coup. Ōtomo Sōrin succeeded his father and moved rapidly against his uncle Kikuchi Yoshitake, who fled to Yatsushiro to seek the help of the Sagara and also raised some support among the *kokujin*, but he was eventually put to death in 1554.[9] Ōtomo Sōrin then went on to raise the family to the peak of their influence, but as far as Higo Province was concerned Sōrin's touch was a light one. Instead of following his father's example and installing a puppet *shugo* or even ruling the province directly himself, Sōrin chose to leave matters in the hands of Higo's *kokujin*, whose vassal status to the Ōtomo appears to have been quite generous. The trusting Sōrin seems to have insisted on little

---

8   Oyama 2003, p. 17.
9   Elisonas 1991, pp. 306–307.

Daimyō Ōtomo Sorin (1530–87) of Bungo Province was one of Japan's most influential kirishitan (Christian) daimy. His family exerted an early influence over the barons of Higo Province, but their touch was light and allowed a considerable independence of action, a state that was threatened by the imposition of Sassa Narimasa in 1587.

more than a regular formal visit to Funai (Bungo's capital) to pay him homage and a willingness to fight for the benevolent Ōtomo family who so generously guaranteed the barons' enviable independence. Otherwise they were allowed to behave as the rulers of their own little kingdoms.[10]

The Ōtomos' paternalistic approach would have been an enviable situation for anyone in Sengoku Japan, but there were two threats to the cosy arrangement. The first was the external danger to Higo Province and the Ōtomo family that was posed by the Shimazu and the Ryūzōji, but at the same time internal problems were caused when the Higo barons took the huge risk of fighting each other and appealing to the greater powers for help, a process that gradually tore apart the 'fire blanket' that the Ōtomo had spread over their province. For example, a long-term rivalry existed between the three Higo baronial families of Jō, Akahoshi and Kumabe, all of whom had once been vassals of the now extinct Kikuchi family. During one dispute with the Kumabe the Akahoshi appealed to the Ōtomo for military help, so Kumabe Chikanaga made an alliance instead with Ōtomo's rival Ryūzōji Takanobu, who invaded Higo Province in 1579 with Chikanaga's support. During that same year Jō Chikamasa of Kumamoto Castle chose to cooperate instead with the Ryūzōji's rivals the Shimazu and allowed them to use Kumamoto as a base for advances against the Kumabe in 1581. In the ninth lunar month of that year a Kumabe army of 2,000 men managed to drive back a Shimazu army of 3,000 from northern Higo, but in 1584 Kumabe's protector Ryūzōji Takanobu was defeated and killed by the Shimazu, so the balance of power changed yet again.[11] The Shimazu soon forced the surrender of the Shōdai, Kumabe, Ōtsuyama, Kōshi and Hebaru barons, leaving the Shimazu as the Higo's overlords in place of the Ōtomo.[12] Fortunately for the barons, the Shimazu turned out to be as generous as the Ōtomo in their attitude to their new subjects, who accepted Shimazu rule with a good grace.

All these machinations, of course, suggest that the concept of a 'floating warrior' went far beyond the personal roles or status of the lower classes and was instead a necessary strategy for a *kokujin*'s survival in which the word 'betrayal' almost had no meaning. The barons' successive periods of service under external *daimyō* control also call into question the true nature of their much-vaunted independence, a matter that drew scorn from J.H. Gubbins in 1880:

---

10 Oyama 2003, p. 129.
11 Araki 1987, p. 76.
12 Araki 1987, p. 15 & pp. 78–79.

Unable to maintain an independent position, these samurai were led by motives of self-preservation to attach themselves to the banner of some noble of the day. And as the fortunes of their patrons changed with the hour, when the ability to protect no longer existed they transferred their allegiance without hesitation to another quarter, and the master of today became the enemy of tomorrow. They had thus no fixed political bias, but were time-servers of necessity, always trimming so as to be on the winning side.[13]

The Floating Ōtsuyama

Gubbins' phrase 'time-servers *of necessity*' should perhaps make us pause and consider how much control the *kokujin* really had over their decision-making. In many cases the arrival of a hostile army would have given them little choice about how to behave, as is illustrated by the classic case-study of the barons from the Ōtsuyama family, whose lands lay near the northern border of Higo, where they controlled two castles: Kamio and Tsuzuragadake, the latter being situated on the summit of the mountain from which the family took its surname.

The Ōtsuyama scheming begins in the year 1550 when, as supporters of the newly restored Kikuchi family, they are found fighting for the puppet Kikuchi Yoshitake against his nephew Ōtomo Sōrin. By 1559, Yoshitake having been disposed of, the current head of the family Ōtsuyama Sukefuyu has changed sides to become the loyal vassal of the Ōtomo and is chastising a rebel on his new master's behalf.[14] In 1578 the Ōtomo are defeated at Mimigawa and their influence declines, so when Ryūzōji Takanobu invades Higo Province in 1579 Ōtsuyama Sukefuyu changes allegiance once again and serves Takanobu by taking the head of someone who has abandoned the Ryūzōji for the Shimazu. Later that same year, however, Sukefuyu throws off his allegiance to the Ryūzōji and shuts himself up in Kamio Castle, which is attacked by the Ryūzōji. Sukefuyu drives them away, taking prisoner seven principal Ryūzōji retainers.[15]

Ōtsuyama Sukefuyu's new-found independence of action seems to be suiting him, because in the fifth month of 1579 Sukefuyu helps a follower of his erstwhile lord Ōtomo against the Ryūzōji. The beneficiary of this new largesse is Kamachi Akihiro, whose castle of Yamashita in Chikugo comes under Ryūzōji attack. Brave Sukefuyu leads a combined force including the Wani of Tanaka to the battle of Shiratori. The fight is indecisive, at which the angry Ryūzōji then besiege Sukefuyu's own castle again, which he defends successfully for five days.[16] Yet in spite of all this noble endeavour on the part of his neighbours Ōtsuyama Sukefuyu can still find the time to increase his own landownings at the expense of others. In July 1580 Sukefuyu joins forces with the Shōdai family and attacks the mountain temple of Kōrasan in

---

13 Gubbins 1880, p. 118.

14 Miyao 2010, p. 25.

15 Miyao 2010, pp. 27–29.

16 Miyao 2010, p. 31; Araki 1987, p. 71.

Chikugo (now the site of Kurume Castle) and throws out its Chief Priest. Two days later, just for good measure, he attacks Kamachi Akihiro in Yamashita Castle, the place he had saved from the Ryūzōji only a year earlier![17]

By 1585 Sukefuyu appears to have 'gone as a guest to the White Jade Pavilion' (a splendid euphemism for dying), leaving his heir Ōtsuyama Iekado to carry on the great family tradition of remorseless self-interest. In that year Hebaru Chikayuki, a baron whose name will feature prominently in the account of Tanaka Castle which follows, becomes the Ōtsuyama's latest target in a dispute over land. Iekado's younger brother Ōtsuyama Ienao attacks Chikayuki's castle of Sakamoto, but when his chief retainer is shot dead by a musket ball the assault force is withdrawn.[18] By now the Shimazu family are the dominant force in Higo, so it is perhaps not surprising to read of Ōtsuyama Iekado moving again from a state of personal independence to service under a new *daimyō*. The Shimazu welcome his change of heart and benefit greatly from Iekado's local knowledge when he becomes a willing guide through Chikugo Province for their major advance against the Ōtomo in 1586. Iekado then leads his own contingent at the Shimazu's siege of Iwaya Castle, where he performs well and receives a letter of commendation from Shimazu Yoshihiro.

Iekado's service to the Shimazu does not last long, because when Toyotomi Hideyoshi invades Kyushu less than a year later he turns his back on the Shimazu and welcomes the conqueror into his castle. Iekado performs the tea ceremony with Hideyoshi and pledges undying loyalty to him, just as he and his father have done on previous occasions to the Kikuchi, Ōtomo, Ryūzōji and Shimazu. One last twist remains however, because when the invasion is over Iekado turns against Hideyoshi in protest at the imposition of Sassa Narimasa on the province, so the last alliances of Iekado's life are made with the Wani and the Hebaru families in the catastrophe of the Higo Rebellion.[19] Iekado finally meets his end at the hands of an assassin during a spurious peace conference and is buried not far from Tanaka Castle.

The above account makes the Ōtsuyama look like the ultimate opportunists, but it is important to note that in turning every new situation to their own advantage they and their fellow floating barons were by no means unique in contemporary Japan, because similar arrangements that involve local *kokujin* taking the part of powerful neighbours and fighting for them from time to time can be identified throughout the Sengoku Period. A very good comparison is to be found in Iga Province (modern Mie Prefecture) where the wide-reaching alliances and campaigns carried out by the Iga *kunishū* would eventually give rise to the legends of the mercenary-like *ninja*.

Where Higo differed from Iga lay in the fact that Higo's *kokujin* never came together as Iga's *kokujin* did to create a formal *ikki*, a league or confederacy of provincial equals whose members pledged support to each other in a written document. The Higo barons were far too independently minded for that, so when we read of the baronial families of Kumabe, Wani, Hebaru

---

17 Miyao 2010, p. 31.
18 Miyao 2010, pp. 35–36.
19 Miyao 2010, p. 39.

The grave of Ōtsuyama Iekado, the archetypal 'floating warrior', is located not far from Tanaka Castle, which was in communication with Iekado's own castle by means of a fire beacon.

and Ōtsuyama taking part in the 1587 Higo Kunishū Ikki the word *ikki* has to be interpreted not as a league but under its other meaning of a revolt or rebellion. There are many references during the Sengoku Period to protesting farmers attacking rice warehouses in violent *ikki* disturbances because of some local grievance, but the Higo Kunishū Ikki was much more than just a spontaneous farmers' riot. It would be one of the fiercest rebellions carried out anytime in Japanese history, an armed reaction by the *kokujin* against the new situation that had developed within their province following Toyotomi Hideyoshi's seemingly all-triumphant Kyushu Campaign of 1587.

3

Hideyoshi's Invasion of Kyushu

Toyotomi Hideyoshi's invasion of Kyushu in 1587 would change the map of Japan forever, sweeping up every *sengoku daimyō* and *kokujin* in its wake as the country moved even further towards reunification. It also marked a great change for Japan's southernmost main island, because for centuries Kyushu had pursued an independent line as the entry point both for new ideas and hostile invasions. Only 40 years earlier Portuguese traders had arrived on Kyushu, bringing the first European muskets ever seen in Japan. They also brought Christianity, which enjoyed some initial success, and one or two of the commanders at Tanaka were *kirishitan daimyō* (Christian lords).

Hideyoshi's Kyushu operation was a large scale one for which the submission of Shikoku in 1585 by means of a seaborne invasion had provided a useful dress rehearsal. He spent the next year planning the massive exercise, which involved marching a huge army along the coast of the Inland Sea and crossing via the narrow Straits of Shinonoseki to defeat the Shimazu of Satsuma, who were determined to secure as much of Kyushu as they could before Hideyoshi's widely heralded invasion arrived. Since the quelling of the Ryūzōji in 1584 the much-weakened Ōtomo had been the Shimazu's prime targets as they moved remorselessly northwards. Having lost much of his territory after the defeat at Mimigawa the current *daimyō* Ōtomo Yoshimune (1558–1610) felt unable to resist the Shimazu on his own, and his desperate request for help from Toyotomi Hideyoshi had provided just the excuse that the latter needed to invade Kyushu on his own behalf.

The Ōtomo realm had not given in easily to the final Shimazu advance. The siege of Iwaya Castle extracted a huge price from the besiegers in both casualties and time, and on Bungo Province's western border Shiga Chikatsugu defended Oka Castle valiantly, while the retired *daimyō* Ōtomo Sōrin employed two Portuguese cannon to hold the castle of Usuki against a division of the Shimazu army that was approaching along the eastern coastal route. However, Ōtomo Yoshimune failed to rise to the standard set by these examples and suffered a crucial defeat at the battle of Hetsugigawa. That opened the gates of Funai Castle to the aggressors, so by the time Hideyoshi had completed his plans of invasion almost the whole of Kyushu had passed under the control of the Shimazu of Satsuma.

To an outside eye the Shimazu appeared unshakeable, but they were tired from their efforts and also perceptive enough to appreciate that something truly massive was on its way. They would no doubt have been heartened by the fact that their victory at Hetsugigawa had included defeating an advance party sent by Toyotomi Hideyoshi, but a decision now had to be made about where to meet the colossal main body that was already making its way along the Inland Sea. The Shimazu accordingly withdrew from the northern provinces of Kyushu by the same routes that they had used so often for attack and took up positions on ground of their own choosing. This was far from being an admission of weakness, because their conquest of northern Kyushu had theoretically given them a number of staunch allies and loyal vassals in the area, whose castles would be defended bravely by those *sengoku daimyō* who had pledged fealty to their impressive neighbours the Shimazu. Furthermore, as natives of Kyushu they too – not to mention the acquiescent *kokujin* in their midst – would naturally be as firmly opposed as the Shimazu were to any takeover of their island by a jumped-up foot soldier from Kyoto.

That was the theory. In fact it took less than a month from the time of his landing for Hideyoshi to crush all opposition. He left Osaka on Tenshō 15, 3m 1d (8 April 1587) and arrived at Kokura Castle in Kyushu on 3m 28d (5 May). As many as 250,000 troops may have made up his total army, which then separated and made its way in two divisions down the eastern and western coasts of Kyushu. Hideyoshi's half-brother Hashiba Hidenaga had to do some real fighting on the eastern approach before recombining with Hideyoshi four weeks later for a final assault on the Shimazu capital of Kagoshima. By contrast, Hideyoshi's march down the western side of Kyushu turned out to be nothing less than a triumphal progress. *Daimyō* who should have opposed him on the Shimazu's behalf submitted meekly.

The *kokujin* of northern Higo quickly saw which way the wind was blowing and rushed to get their cards marked as supporters of Hideyoshi, so any alliances with or submissions to the Shimazu were quickly forgotten. On 4m 12d (19 May) Hideyoshi chose Nankan as a place to rest on his unhurried way south, so the local barons gained a welcome audience with him.[1] According to tradition Hideyoshi performed the tea ceremony at a local temple, and the spring from which the water was taken for the ritual is proudly preserved to this day below the hill of Ōtsuyama.[2] The local *kokujin* Ōtsuyama Iekado, who so recently had fought for the Shimazu at Iwaya Castle, offered to join the attack on the Shimazu but received the reply that Hideyoshi preferred him to stay in charge of his vital border fortress.[3] Other barons carried out token attacks on the Shimazu as the army retreated through their territories, or at the very least claimed that they had done so. For example, the Satsuma general Miyahara Kagetane is known to have died fighting as he withdrew from Kumanoshō Castle. When the *kokujin* Akahoshi and Nawa submitted to Hideyoshi at Kumanoshō they claimed

---

1   Oyama 2003, p. 53.
2   Miyao 2010, p. 96.
3   Araki 1987, p. 16.

that it was they who had killed the general.[4] The Kumabe family also seem to have joined Hideyoshi's advance with their armed *kunishū* and may even have invaded Satsuma on Hideyoshi's behalf.[5]

Wani Chikazane, whose castle of Tanaka would shortly come under attack, was the most insistent of all about his part in defeating the Shimazu. *Wani Gundan* claims that he was the first to cross the Satsuma border, where he 'performed meritorious military service' and was rewarded by being confirmed by Hideyoshi in his existing landholdings.[6] Similar claims to this provided the background to the argument the barons would later use against the imposition of an overlord. As a result of their pledge to serve Hideyoshi and their bravery on his behalf, they maintained, he had assured them that their existing landownings would be honoured. More than that, Hideyoshi is supposed to have guaranteed their status in writing by means of an official red-seal letter issued at Nankan. Unfortunately this vital document does not appear to have survived in any form.

The Shimazu's retreat through Higo Province was hastened by Hideyoshi's new-found allies who had once been worsted by the Shimazu, among whom was Ryūzōji Masaie (1556–1607), son of the late Takanobu. He showed his enthusiasm for Hideyoshi by entering Higo and presenting a show of force against Takaba Castle, which was still held on the Shimazu's behalf by the *kokujin* Kōshi in a rare example of steadfast loyalty. Kōshi refused to surrender until he was forcefully persuaded in that direction by the use of a large cannon.[7] Ryūzōji Masaie then besieged the much more important Yatsushiro Castle. The Shimazu sent an army and succeeded in relieving it, but suffered so much harassment from the vengeful Sagara that this vital strategic fortress was soon abandoned.

The Satsuma army then pulled out of Higo for the last time and entered their home province almost as fugitives.[8] Having also suffered serious defeats in Hyūga Province at the hands of Hashiba Hidenaga, and faced with the promise of the recombination of a large and confident expeditionary force and the prospect of the largest mass suicide in Japanese history, their *daimyō* Shimazu Yoshihisa (1533–1611) had his head shaved as a sign of his withdrawal from the world and journeyed to the invaders' headquarters on 5m 8d (13 June). There he accepted submission as Hideyoshi's vassal. The largest military expedition in Japanese history had come to a satisfactory conclusion.

Magnanimous in achieving victory and realistic in the means of sustaining it, Hideyoshi left the humiliated Shimazu in control of Satsuma and Ōsumi Provinces while confiscating all their other domains. The Ōtomo family, on whose behalf the Kyushu Campaign had ostensibly been fought, were likewise left in charge of Bungo, while the nearby Arima, Matsuura and

---

4   Araki 1987, p. 17.

5   Araki 1987, p. 17.

6   The claim also appears in the records of the Ono family, to whom the Wani were related. See Kunitake 1993, p. 115.

7   Araki 1987, p. 80; Araki 2012, p. 72.

8   Gubbins 1880, p. 119.

Ryūzōji *daimyō*, all of whom had regarded Hideyoshi as the lesser of two evils and submitted to him with alacrity, were also re-assigned to their existing territories. In Higo Province Kuma District was reconfirmed as the domain of the incumbent Sagara Yorifusa (1574–1636), whose family had suffered so much from the Shimazu,[9] while other *daimyō* were moved around within Kyushu to guarantee the island's future security like so many potted plants inside a greenhouse.

In making these land transfers Toyotomi Hideyoshi was merely demonstrating a successful model of post-war resettlement that Oda Nobunaga had introduced several years earlier, which involved controlling recalcitrant provinces by giving them new *daimyō* who were appointed from within

The Shimazu family surrendered to Toyotomi Hideyoshi at the end of his invasion of Kyushu. Within months Hideyoshi's hard-won authority on Japan's great southern island was to be challenged by the Higo Rebellion.

the ranks of his most loyal generals. It was a process that had the added advantage of separating a *daimyō* from any traditional local sympathies, thus ensuring that future rebellions were less likely to occur. Some Kyushu *daimyō* who had lost castles to the Shimazu and then fought for Hideyoshi were included in the scheme and were found new domains of increased size. For example Tachibana Muneshige (1567–1642), who had lost Tachibana Castle in Chikuzen, was given Yanagawa Castle in Chikugo.

Other 'potted plants' would be coming to live in Kyushu for the first time in their lives, and the most prominent example of these was Kobayakawa Takakage (1533–97). He was the third son of Mōri Motonari (1497–1571) the *sengoku daimyō* of Aki Province (modern Hiroshima Prefecture) who had raised the family to a position of pre-eminence in the general area of the Inland Sea until his grandson was forced to make peace with Hideyoshi in 1582. Takakage received a large 307,000 *koku* domain centred on Najima Castle in Chikuzen Province. Similarly, Kobayakawa Takakage's younger brother and adopted heir Mōri Hidekane (1567–1601), who was one of Japan's *kirishitan daimyō,* was given the 75,000 *koku* domain of Kurume Castle in Chikugo. Among the other names who feature prominently in the literature relating to Tanaka we note Mōri Yoshinari (?–1611), who was granted Kokura Castle and a 60,000 *koku* domain.[10]

---

9   Araki 2012, p. 144.

10 He was ordered by Hideyoshi to change his surname to Mori and appears in the accounts of the Higo Rebellion as Mori Iki-no-Kami. 'Iki-no-Kami' is an example of a common honorific title

These incomers' new subjects were forced to accept their new *daimyō* for old ones, but elsewhere in Kyushu certain lower-class inhabitants of the great southern island who had supposedly been spared *daimyō* rule suddenly found themselves under the control of a *daimyō* for the first time. Higo was a case in point, and its *kokujin* barons held their breath while the major programme of reorganisation began to unfold around them. Surely their bravery and self-sacrifice against the Shimazu, not to mention the enthusiastic welcome they had given to their liberator the mighty Toyotomi Hideyoshi, would have ensured the continuation of the status quo granted by the Ōtomo and sustained under the Shimazu? It was not to be. Instead of handing out rewards for their help in driving out the retreating Shimazu forces, Hideyoshi imposed outside control upon the barons in the person of a general called Sassa Narimasa (1539–88).

Sassa Narimasa was transferred from Etchū Province (modern Toyama Prefecture) to a newly created fief that consisted of 13 districts out of the 14 that made up Higo Province. There are no records of its assessed wealth at the time, although figures from a survey done about 20 years earlier on behalf of the last Ashikaga shogun had valued the whole of Higo at the equivalent of 340,220 *koku*.[11] In having Narimasa imposed upon it Higo Province was of course being treated no differently from the rest of Kyushu or indeed from the rest of Japan, but in most other places the process had effectively meant the replacement of one existing and often unpopular *daimyō* by another, not the loss of a cherished independence of action enjoyed by proud local barons who (theoretically at least) had never had to suffer any *daimyō*, good, bad, or indifferent.

Hideyoshi's imposition of a similar means of military control throughout the country over the next three years marked the shift from Medieval to Early Modern Japan, and meant that Japan began to emerge from what Hall calls 'the period of its greatest political fragmentation into what was to be its most successful centralisation prior to modern times'.[12] Hideyoshi would eventually strengthen the local political settlements by enacting a very thorough standardised nationwide land survey, and carrying out his *katana gari* (Sword Hunt) whereby all villagers, farmers, seafarers and priests were disarmed. The latter operation would be crucial for securing the separation of the military and the farming classes which would one day characterise Tokugawa Japan.[13] All these actions were major shifts in policy, and in his study of the age Hall reminds us that the political and domestic reforms by Hideyoshi 'are well known…, have been abundantly studied' and are 'described in great detail'.[14] What is missing from this great wealth

---

given to a *daimyō*. The suffix means 'protector of' the province that makes up the first part of the name. In most cases the recipient of the title had no connections with the province he was supposed to be protecting. Sassa Narimasa, for example, was Mutsu-no-Kami, 'protector' of Mutsu Province in the far north of Japan.

11 Oyama 2003, p. 39.
12 Hall 1981, p. 7.
13 For a full account of the Sword Hunt see Fujiki H, 2005. *Katanagari*. Tokyo: Iwanami Shoten.
14 Hall 1981, p. 194.

Daimyō Sassa Narimasa (1539–1588) is the villain of the Higo Rebellion. Hideyoshi appointed him as daimyō under strict instructions not to enrage the kokujin, and the subsequent revolt was the result of his mismanagement. This life-sized dummy of him was formerly in Kiyosu Castle as part of a diorama showing him in attendance on Oda Nobunaga.

of scholarly material, however, is much recognition of the opposition the measures provoked.

The Higo Rebellion illustrates very well how Hideyoshi's reunification programme was intended to destroy all the independent *sengoku daimyō* along with any remaining independent *kokujin*, and the devastating sequence of events that occurred in the province between 1587 and 1588 shows this nationwide process in poignant microcosm. In *The Cambridge History of Japan* Jurgis Elisonas refers accurately and succinctly to Hideyoshi's invasion of Kyushu as 'the finale of the long drama of Kyushu as a place with an independent identity in Japanese history'. The Higo Rebellion, which Elisonas calls the 'last flare up of the lost independence' was its sequel, and the siege of Tanaka Castle would become the flare's fiercest burning flame.[15]

---

15 Elisonas 1991, pp. 358–359.

4

Sassa Narimasa and the Higo Rebellion

Sassa Narimasa's appointment to Higo Province is described as follows in *Taikō-ki*, an elaborate fictionalised version of the life of Toyotomi Hideyoshi that was published in 1625:

> On 6m 1d (6 July 1587) [Hideyoshi] left Yatsushiro in Higo Province for Kumamoto; during his stay on about the second day, because Higo was a large province, Sassa Mutsu-no-Kami Narimasa was appointed *shugo* of Higo. Sassa was greatly honoured by this.[1]

Higo's new *daimyō* had led a charmed life. Once described unfairly by the Japanese historian Tokutomi as having the military acumen of 'a dried sardine gnashing its teeth',[2] Sassa Narimasa had a distinguished military record in charge of one of Oda Nobunaga's two élite Horse Guards units and had shared command of the arquebus troops at the famous battle of Nagashino in 1575. He was granted the domain of Etchū Province and based himself in the castle of Toyama, but following Nobunaga's death Narimasa made the wrong choice and took sides against the up-and-coming Toyotomi Hideyoshi. In 1584 Narimasa attacked Suemori Castle, which was held by the pro-Hideyoshi general Maeda Toshiie. Thoroughly defeated, Sassa Narimasa made a forced march across bitterly cold snow-covered mountains to seek support – a heroic trek much celebrated in Japanese art – only to be rejected and forced to suffer a humiliating surrender to Hideyoshi's army. Quite unexpectedly, Hideyoshi then pardoned him, so a relieved Narimasa entered Hideyoshi's service and played an honourable role in the invasion of Kyushu. This must have redeemed him in Hideyoshi's eyes, and Elizabeth Berry, in her biography of Hideyoshi, sees the award of Higo as an attempt to heal wounds with a former 'defiant peer in the Oda army'.[3]

---

1 Yoshida Y. (ed.), *Taikō-ki* Volume II (Tokyo, Kyōikusha, 1979), pp. 189–190.
2 Quoted in Sadler, A.L., *The Maker of Modern Japan: The Life of Tokugawa Ieyasu* (London: Allen and Unwin, 1937), p. 134.
3 Berry, Mary Elizabeth, *Hideyoshi* (Cambridge Mass: Harvard University Press, 1982), p. 91.

The lucky Sassa Narimasa took up residence in Kumamoto Castle on Tenshō 15, 6m 6d (11 July 1587). It was the first time in its history that Kumamoto had become a provincial capital, although his castle was not the magnificent palace fortress that dominates the city today. That castle dates from 1611; Narimasa's base was a much simpler place on an adjacent site. From there he proceeded to rule his new domain, and as Hideyoshi's army completed its withdrawal from Kyushu the barons of Higo awaited developments with considerable trepidation. What they did not know was that if Narimasa had gone on to obey Hideyoshi's orders to the letter they would have had little to fear, because Narimasa's terms of reference required from him a very gentle touch. Hideyoshi may not have wanted to return the barons to their medieval state of opportunistic quasi-independence, but he was certainly not willing to cause undue resentment for the time being. Mighty Kyushu had been pacified and that peace had to continue, so the plan Hideyoshi had in mind was not too different from the paternalistic approach once exercised by the Ōtomo and the Shimazu. This was made very clear in the words of Narimasa's appointment, which were set out within a red-seal letter from Hideyoshi on 6m 6d (11 July):

In this print Sassa Narimasa is shown in a heroic – albeit rebellious – role during the winter of 1584. Being desperate to persuade Tokugawa Ieyasu to return to the fray against Hideyoshi after his defeat at Nagakute, Narimasa crossed the Zara Pass in the Tateyama mountain range under deep snow. His daring journey to Hamamatsu Castle proved unsuccessful, and even though his bravery and dash endeared him to other lords, their lukewarm support was not enough to prevent Hideyoshi from defeating Narimasa at Toyama in 1585.

Item, you are to grant to the fifty-two *kokujin* the lands they formerly possessed.
Item, you are not to undertake a land survey until after three years have passed.
Item, it is important that the farmers should not suffer any hardship.
Item, you must take care that no revolts (*ikki*) occur.
Item, you will be excused from any building projects in the Kamigata area (Kyoto-Osaka) for three years.
It is a central principle that there must be no variation from the above provisions concerning that to which you have been appointed. Thus it is.

Tenshō 15, 6m 6d (red-seal)
Sassa Kuranosuke *dono*.[4]

Had Sassa Narimasa stuck to the terms of the agreement he could have passed himself off as Higo's benevolent new master and might even have been loved by his grateful subjects for three years at least. For their part, the *kokujin* would have been confirmed in their landownings in return for recognising

---

4   Oyama 2003, p. 75.

Narimasa as *daimyō*, and in view of how they had readily pledged allegiance to the Ōtomo and Shimazu in the past, that should not have been too difficult a pill to swallow. Yet there was one new and very important factor to consider. The Shimazu, Ryūzōji and Ōtomo had accepted vassalage from the petty rulers of Higo without any need to occupy their province, but Sassa Narimasa had been moved from distant Etchū along with all his household and senior retainers. His followers had been uprooted after serving Narimasa in battle and expected new lands as a reward for their services. Hideyoshi must have foreseen this because of his insistence on no land assessment being carried out in Higo for three years, but it was not long before the barons' fears about Sassa Narimasa were justified, because he immediately began a land survey in complete contravention of Hideyoshi's orders.

As the *kokujin* had suspected, this detailed operation was not merely an exercise in agrarian economics but a preliminary step towards Narimasa rewarding his own retainers with the barons' lands, which were of course the only ones available. Ōtsuyama Iekado, for example, would see his domain slashed from 307 *chō* to 50 *chō* as a result of the exercise. It was a far cry from the hands-off approach once exercised by Ōtomo Sōrin. Believing that their ancient independence was under threat, the *kokujin* expressed serious displeasure, arguing that they had served Hideyoshi well during the Kyushu campaign, and also stating most forcibly that Hideyoshi had confirmed their status quo in writing, but when no concessions came, Iekado and his fellow sufferers took up arms against Sassa Narimasa. Over the course of the following year sporadic uprisings, attacks on supply columns and sieges of tiny hilltop castles would challenge Hideyoshi's hard-won authority on Kyushu in the form of the Higo Rebellion.

Sassa Narimasa was not without some local support. At his peer level Sagara Yorifusa, with whom he shared Higo, backed Narimasa completely and prevented any possible insurrection within Kuma District but, more importantly, the revolt did not attract total commitment inside the *kokujin* ranks. A few of the barons did not rebel and fought instead for Sassa Narimasa throughout the campaign, hoping no doubt that faithful service to a new master – a concept by no means alien to a floating warrior – would bring reward, but most of them did not accept the new regime in such a gentlemanly fashion.

To add to the objectors' discomfort, the move towards *daimyō* control of Higo Province that most of the *kokujin* opposed so violently involved much more than just a loss of independence to Narimasa and a loss of land to his retainers. It also heralded a historic shift from their dual status as fighting samurai and productive landowners towards a choice having to be made between one or the other. For those who became samurai the process would ultimately result in the transformation of the military class to 'landless, urban-living stipendiaries'.[5] This new breed of samurai would live in castle towns rather than in the countryside and would be paid a stipend for service in a *daimyō*'s army rather than having to derive an income from land ownership

---

5   Hall 1981, p. 207.

and its cultivation. By contrast, those *jizamurai* who were denied the status of samurai were forced to stay behind in the villages, a firm distinction that would be given dramatic effect from September 1588 onwards by the forceful disarmament of villagers under the Sword Hunt. Deprived of weapons with which to defend themselves, the full-time farmers had to accept a new status under samurai control.

The status of being a full-time samurai who lived in a castle and enjoyed the military life would have had obvious attractions for an aspiring warrior, hence Hall's comment that many *jizamurai* were only too happy to move out of the countryside and take up residence at their *daimyō*'s headquarters.[6] In Kyushu some very successful moves towards separation are illustrated by the settlement made in Chikuzen Province on behalf of its new *daimyō* Kobayakawa Takakage. Chikuzen's former *jizamurai* Sōzō and Asai had their lands removed and entered the service of Takakage as his *yoriki*. The word would later mean a particular rank within the Tokugawa samurai class who acted as Edo's police force, but in 1587 it simply meant a samurai. In other words, the *jizamurai* of Chikuzen had lost their *ji*.

In one possibly unique case within Sassa's newly acquired lands in Higo the *jizamurai* family of Harada gave up their lands voluntarily and became Narimasa's *yoriki*.[7] Yet they were notable exceptions, because most of the barons of Higo Province were not ready for the separation process either economically or emotionally. It might have been acceptable if they had been the lords who were directing the operation. Indeed, they would probably have liked to have taken their own *jizamurai* into their exclusively military service in the baronial halls if only they could have afforded the loss in productive capacity that such a move would entail. That would have meant a rise in status for everyone, but upward social mobility was not on the agenda of Sassa Narimasa, who envisaged the barons becoming his stipendiary retainers like the Harada. Yet their leaders said no, and constantly reminded anyone who would listen to them that the proud barons of Higo had enjoyed a personal audience with Hideyoshi at Nankan to confirm their status and had even joined him for the tea ceremony, a ritual that was almost a definition of one's acceptance into polite society. The *kokujin* may have been less well off financially than Narimasa but they were his equal in pride and personal ambition, and when faced with his duplicity they set in motion the other traditional role associated with a *sengoku daimyō* and went to war to defend their own interests.

From Jōmura to Kumamoto

The initial ringleader of the Higo Rebellion was Kumabe Chikanaga. He is revered to this day as a local hero, as is shown in no uncertain fashion by the large bronze statue of him that was unveiled in Kikuchi in 2011. It is equal in height to the statue of Katō Kiyomasa, the famous *daimyō* of Kumamoto

---

6   Hall 1981, p. 212.
7   Oyama 1993, p. 63.

The ringleader of the Higo Rebellion was Kumabe Chikanaga. He is revered to this day as a local hero, as shown in no uncertain fashion by this large bronze statue of him that was unveiled in Kikuchi in 2011. His mon (family badge) of a fan-design is shown on his jacket.

Castle, whose image has long loomed over the city of Kumamoto. In 1587 the Kumabe family controlled three major strongpoints. The first was the Kumabe Yakata or Kumabe Mansion, which was defended from a distance by the purely military installation of Nagano Castle (otherwise known as Sarugaeki) with which it shared a mountain. The other two places were Jōmura Castle on a hill to the north of modern Yamaga City and Waifu Castle, the site of which is the Kikuchi Shrine in Kikuchi City. Waifu, which had once been the headquarters of the glorious but ill-fated Kikuchi family, became the first flashpoint for the Higo Rebellion.[8]

Believing, not unreasonably, that he could nip Kumabe Chikanaga's revolt in the bud, Sassa Narimasa sent an army of 6,000 men to attack Waifu Castle on 7m 24d (27 August 1587). The main gate was defended by a retainer of the Kumabe called Taku Munesada whom Narimasa secretly persuaded to betray his master.[9] Munesada set fire to the gate, and with no prospect of a relieving army arriving, the castle surrendered three days later on 7m 27d (30 August).[10] Chikanaga fled to the protection of his son Kumabe Chikayasu in Jōmura.

In the meantime Sassa Narimasa had defeated Chikanaga's retainer Yūdō Kanemoto at Nagano, after which both victor and vanquished headed for Jōmura. Kanemoto joined the defenders while Sassa Narimasa began a siege of Jōmura on 8m 7d (10 September 1587), setting up his headquarters in the nearby Buddhist temple of Nichirinji, from where there was a good view of his target.[11] With two defeated rebel castles already under his belt, Narimasa no doubt expected another quick victory. In fact, Jōmura Castle would keep up a fierce resistance throughout the entire Higo Rebellion, and it was partly for this reason that Hideyoshi would put so many resources into destroying Tanaka Castle when the Wani barons joined in with the revolt. The loss of Tanaka would cut Jōmura off from support, a strategy that ultimately proved true because Jōmura only capitulated after Tanaka had been destroyed.

---

8   Araki 2012, p. 52. It is interesting to note that the museum within the treasure house of the Kikuchi Shrine concentrates totally on the Kikuchi family and ignores the Kumabe completely, with no reference being made anywhere to the Higo Rebellion. It is perhaps not surprising that no artefacts should have survived from the rebellious family, but their mere existence seems to have been airbrushed from Kikuchi City.

9   Oyama 2003, p. 85.

10   Kunitake 1993, p. 105.

11   Araki 2012, p. 58

A document called *Jōmura shusen ki* (Chronicle of the defensive war of Jōmura) produced during the Edo Period gives a precise breakdown of the large number of people who packed themselves into the complex structure of earthworks and palisades that made up Jōmura Castle. It reads as follows:

Men and women:	Above 15,000
Of which men	Above 8,000
Women and children	Above 7,000
Samurai	Above 800
Muskets	830 (among which 100 are with the *ukimusha*)
Bows	505 (among which 100 are with the *ukimusha*)[12]

The document goes on to give the names of the defending unit commanders and their nearest castle gateway. The presence of many non-combatants during a siege is completely understandable, so the figures are probably not exaggerated even though the numbers of women and children greatly outnumber the fighting men, whose ranks include first of all warriors referred to as samurai. The figures given for muskets and bows must also mean the men who were trained to wield them as well as the weapons themselves because they are distinguished from the samurai, who must be regarded as fighters with edged weapons rather than a strict group definition based on social class or wealth. There is however the additional unit known as *ukimusha*, who appear to exist outside the samurai class, loosely defined though it was. Yūdō Magoshichi is their *ukimusha kashira* (*ukimusha* captain), a statement which further implies that the *ukimusha* were regarded as a separate category of warrior.[13]

Sassa Narimasa quickly came to appreciate the strength of Jōmura Castle, because he attacked it immediately on the day of his arrival on 10 September and was decisively repulsed. Araki notes that *Kumabe Monogatari* mentions that Yūdō Magoshichi in particular encouraged his *ukimusha* towards fierce fighting.[14] Having been prevented from achieving a early victory, Narimasa ordered a siege on the following day 8m 8d (11 September), but he did so in a radical departure from the usual pattern of setting up encircling lines around a castle. This was because Jōmura simply covered too large an area. It was built on an isolated hill among flatlands and was so well situated that Narimasa was forced to build two castles of his own about 400 metres from each other on its southern side.[15] They were known as the Eastern and Western *tsukejiro* 付城, which simply means a support castle built by a besieger to use against the defended castle.[16] The best analogy would be to compare them to redoubts, the entrenched strongpoints built, for example, during the Crimean War, but Jōmura's 'western redoubt' and 'eastern redoubt' were comparable in size to

12 Mikawa 1997, p. 210. A version with slightly different numbers appears in Araki 2012, pp. 57–58.
13 Araki 2012, p. 58.
14 Araki 1987, p. 49.
15 Tanaka Hiroshi, 2004, 'Go-aisatsu' *Sengoku da yori* 4, p. 1.
16 Kunitake 1993, p. 103; Miyao 2010, p. 43.

This reconstructed bridge, ditch and fence at Hachigata Castle show typical simple defences that would have been present at both Jōmura and Tanaka, where use was made of timber and earthworks.

any small contemporary Japanese castle. The Nishi-Tsukejiro held 180 men and the Higashi-Tsukejiro held 170 men.[17] Stationed in the lines between the two places was Shōdai Chikayasu, one of the few *kokujin* who had remained loyal to Narimasa.[18]

On 8m 13d (16 September) Narimasa launched a general attack on Jōmura from the two *tsukejiro* but lost 78 men in the process, including a relative called Sassa Ubanosuke.[19] He had now been repulsed twice from the place, and when the news spread throughout the *kokujin*, other rebel armies took advantage of the situation and raised the flag of revolt in their own territories. Ōtsuyama Iekado, for example, challenged Sassa's local representative and fortified his own castles.[20] In the opposite direction from Jōmura the Uchikoga family rebelled at Shimono Castle in the Ueki District.

These actions will be described in a later chapter, because Sassa Narimasa did not send armies against them immediately. The reason was that a far more serious development had occurred nearer to home, because a group of *kokujin* had dared to exploit Narimasa's absence and boldly attacked his headquarters of Kumamoto Castle.[21] He had left it in the capable hands of Jimbō Ujiharu, an Etchū man who had followed his master to Higo after

---

17 Araki 2012, p. 61.
18 Araki 2012, p. 61.
19 Nagabayashi, Shōin *Hōsatsu gunki. Hisatsu gunkishū* (Tokyo: Rekishi Toshosha 1980), p. 106.
20 Araki 1987, p. 42.
21 Araki 2012, pp. 45 & 53; Oyama 2003, pp. 85–86.

In this painting in the Nagashino Castle Preservation Hall two simply dressed warriors are defending a position behind an openwork fence. The jizamurai at Tanaka would have looked very similar to these characters.

years of devoted service. The attack on Kumamoto Castle was carried out by various Higo *kokujin*, among whom a prominent role was taken by Kai Sōryū of Mifune Castle. Much of the fighting at Kumamoto involved Jimbō Ujiharu's men making heroic sallies out of its gates against the besiegers, but Ujiharu was so hard pressed that Narimasa was forced to leave the siege lines at Jōmura to assist him.

The Sassa army had to travel to Kumamoto with great care because the countryside between Yamaga and Kumamoto was in uproar, so Narimasa divided his forces for the march. He himself headed for Kumamoto by a circuitous route via Kōshi and arrived safely on 8m 15d (18 September), while his unfortunate nephew Sassa Muneyoshi took the main road to Kumamoto through Ueki and Kanokogi with 300 horsemen. Muneyoshi's army may have been intended as a decoy force, but *Shimono raiyū ki* relates what happened when they were spotted:

When Muneyoshi's force approached the Ueki area the sight of men and women from the neighbouring villages gave the impression that they were probably local samurai in martial array. The scouts in Muneyoshi's vanguard saw them and mistook them for soldiers waiting in ambush. They reported it to Muneyoshi, who made a detour to avoid these people. Many of the Uchikoga retainers saw this, and the local warriors thought they were cowards and opened fire on them on a whim, hitting mounted men so that samurai fell from their horses. On seeing this happen Muneyoshi ordered an advance to repel the ambushing troops. However, Muneyoshi's force, who had no knowledge of the local geography, came under musket fire from cover and were killed at the hands of the Uchikoga troops. A few stragglers made it to Kanokogi, but there was hardly one horseman left behind except Muneyoshi. Muneyoshi went into a wood and is said to have committed suicide.[22]

The chronicle goes on to describe how Sassa Muneyoshi behaved like the samurai heroes of old and sat down on his armour skirt to cut his abdomen open in a classic act of ritual suicide. He was buried on the battlefield, for which his recently refurbished grave provides the only marker.

Sassa Narimasa may have lost half of his army at Ueki, but he still possessed an unusual trump card in the defence of Kumamoto Castle, because it contained two young hostages who had been sent there on Hideyoshi's explicit instructions. They were the heirs of the family of the Daigūji (Chief Priest) of the Aso Shrine, an institution that was held in great reverence by the people of Higo. The position was a hereditary one within the family, who

The recently refurbished grave of Sassa Narimasa's unfortunate nephew Sassa Muneyoshi, who was ambushed here on the road from Yamaga to Kumamoto by troops from the Uchikoga family. Muneyoshi committed seppuku in classic samurai style.

---

22 Araki 1987, pp. 57–58.

had once enjoyed a formidable military reputation to add to their religious charisma. By 1587, however, the family had suffered from various incursions into Higo and the current Daigūji, Aso Koreteru (1582–93), was only five years old; his brother Koreyoshi (1583–1663) was four. They provided an important deterrent against an attack on the castle by the Higo *kunishū*, particularly those from the Aso District. The Watanabe family, for example, who had once been members of the old Aso warrior band, decided not to rebel but to provide assistance to Narimasa merely to save Kumamoto from going up in flames and taking their sacred heir with it.[23]

A further group of barons also stayed loyal to Narimasa and assisted his entry into Kumamoto by launching a surprise rear attack on their fellow *kunishū* at the castle's main gate.[24] This loyalist army went under the general name of the Yamanoue Sannashu-shū (the three families from the top of the mountain) who owned lands around Kimpusan, a mountain to the north-west of Kumamoto. Their names were Tajiri, Ukushima and Uchida. Before Narimasa's arrival they had owned lands valued at 500 *chō*. On his arrival in Higo Narimasa had allocated 250 *chō* to them, but instead of rebelling they followed the example of Shōdai Chikayasu and placed their trust in the rewards that would follow good service. So it was to prove, with an additional 50 *chō* being allocated to them following their assistance in the defence of Kumamoto.[25] On 8m 28d (30 September) Narimasa granted a further 170 *chō* to the Yamanoue Sannashu-shū in recognition of their fighting at Kumamoto and on 10m 1d (1 November) Narimasa increased their holdings again by 21 *chō*.

Sassa Narimasa's relieving army arrived at Kumamoto Castle and fell upon the rebels outside it, at which Kai Sōryū was severely wounded and the castle was saved.[26] Kumamoto was never attacked again during the entire rebellion, although the two Aso brothers would stay there as hostages even after the Higo Rebellion had finished because the sacred nature of their lineage still had the potential to spark further revolt. Two days after the lifting of the threat a satisfied Narimasa returned to Jōmura Castle, where the long siege was winding on. By the beginning of the ninth month the two *tsukejiro* were beginning

The armour of Tachibana Muneshige (1567-1642), who played a major role in the Higo Rebellion after his supply column to Jōmura came under attack. He was involved in the first assault on Tanaka Castle, which passed under his temporary ownership once the siege was over.

---

23 Araki 1987, p. 62.
24 Araki 1987, p. 61.
25 Araki 1987, pp. 61–62.
26 Araki 2012, pp. 62–63

to run out of supplies, so on 9m 7d (8 October) Narimasa requested Tachibana Muneshige of Yanagawa Castle to send relief. Three rebel *kunishū* consisting of 300 men in total planned an attack on the pack horse column, but their timing went awry. Because of this they were too late to prevent the supplies going in, and when they attacked Tachibana's column on its return journey near Hirano the rebels came off worse and were driven away. The names of the three *kokujin* families involved in the raid were Ōtsuyama, Hebaru and Wani. With that operation the Wani family took part in the Higo Rebellion for the first time, and the reversal led them to expect an imminent attack on their own fortress of Tanaka Castle.[27]

---

27 Oyama 2003, pp. 93–94; Araki 2012, pp. 65–66.

5

Hideyoshi's Call to Arms

One of the most popular myths about the Higo Rebellion involves the moment when Hideyoshi heard about what was happening to Sassa Narimasa. The opening scene of the movie *Kumamoto Monogatari* follows the melodramatic version, whereby the bad news arrives during a grand tea ceremony staged by Hideyoshi at the Kitano Tenmangū, a shrine in northern Kyoto. This historical event, which began on 10m 1d (1 November 1587) was a unique and lavish spectacle whereby Hideyoshi, a devotee of the ritual of tea, had invited anybody who was anybody to join him and be stunned by his aesthetic accomplishments. The rarest and finest tea implements were on show and the most exquisite practitioners of the tea ceremony were in attendance to assist Hideyoshi in his masterly performance. Some lucky visitors (chosen by lottery) were even served tea by the great man himself, and no doubt returned to their homes speechless with admiration.

The first day of the Kitano Tea Ceremony began well, with Hideyoshi personally serving tea to 803 guests, but he then returned to his palace and the rest of the event was cancelled. Elison suggests sensibly that the ceremony was curtailed simply because Hideyoshi was tired or that the reaction by his guests had not been as fulsome as he had desired.[1] The alternative explanation depicted in the movie shows a messenger arriving the middle of the aesthetic spectacle to inform Hideyoshi that the Higo barons have revolted and that Sassa Narimasa is unable to control them. Hideyoshi then flies into a rage at this embarrassing reversal to his triumph in Kyushu. Generals are sent packing from the tea house with orders to crush the revolt, and a priceless tea bowl ends up in smithereens on the floor, flung to the ground by a furious Hideyoshi.

In reality, the dates of the relevant letters from Hideyoshi to his generals show that by the time of the Great Kitano Tea Ceremony the operation to crush the rebellion had been under way for nearly two months, so it cannot have been hot news. In all probability, the first Hideyoshi knew about the Higo Rebellion was by reports from Kyushu sent by Kuroda Yoshitaka and Mori Iki-no-Kami, as would be confirmed later in a letter written to Hideyoshi by

---

1   Elison, George and Smith, Bardwell L. (eds.), *Warlords, Artists and Commoners: Japan in the Sixteenth Century* (Honolulu: University of Hawaii Press, 1981), pp. 239–240.

Kobayakawa Takakage on 7m 23d (26 August). It is nonetheless more than likely that the annoyance Hideyoshi expressed when he read Kobayakawa's letter reflected the fury portrayed in the popular myth. He was however level-headed and pragmatic in his approach, because the resettlement of the Kyushu domains under his most loyal generals meant that another invasion was not needed. There were already enough *daimyō* on Kyushu within a short marching distance of Higo Province who could assist the incompetent and disobedient Sassa Narimasa, so Hideyoshi wrote back immediately placing Kobayakawa Takakage in overall command of crushing the rebellion. Takakage was given no specific instructions at that stage, just an order to monitor the situation:

> I saw your letter of the 23rd when I arrived in Kyoto today. The Kumabe business in the letter is exactly as it was related by Kuroda Kangeyu and Mori Iki-no-Kami. I have entrusted the affairs of both provinces to you; they have rebelled and in line with your report it seems that you must be prepared to cut off some heads. In connection with this, give some thought to the building of castles and be on your guard.[2]

The siege of Jōmura began the day after this letter was written. Hideyoshi was kept informed of developments there and at Kumamoto, and on 9m 7d (8 October), the same day that Tachibana's supply column was being attacked by the Wani and Hebaru barons, Hideyoshi dictated a second letter to Kobayakawa Takakage ordering him to get closer to the action by basing

Kobayakawa Takakage (1533–97) was entrusted by Hideyoshi with the task of crushing the Higo Rebellion. This very serious-looking statue of him stands on the site of his castle of Mihara on the Inland Sea.

---

2   Oyama 2003, pp. 84–85.

himself in his brother's Kurume Castle. In the letter Hideyoshi is also very critical of Sassa Narimasa:

> I am forwarding this red-seal letter promptly to Sassa Mutsu-no-Kami's location; I saw your letter of the 18th day of last month. As for the matter of Higo Province, my understanding is that Narimasa has carried out poor government of the *kunishū* and the farmers so that they have risen recklessly in revolt. Assemble the commanders and soldiers of Higo and Chikugo and provide assistance to Sassa Mutsu-no-Kami.
>
> Kobayakawa Takakage will depart for Kurume castle in Chikugo, investigate the state of affairs and take command, and all must obey him in this; Kuroda Kangeyu and Mori Iki-no-Kami will take charge in his absence when he sets off to war.
>
> Therefore, Takakage, depart for war as soon as circumstances permit; be on your guard and make your arrangements quickly.
>
> I have sent an identical letter to Ryūzōji Masaie.[3]

Hideyoshi wrote a third letter to Kobayakawa Takakage the next day. As the following extract shows, Hideyoshi is looking at the overall strategic situation including the possibility of moving extra troops into Higo if it should become necessary. He also stresses the need to maintain defences in northern Kyushu in case the Higo Rebellion should spread to other provinces:

> This will also be forwarded promptly to Mutsu-no-Kami, identified by the honourable vermilion seal. I saw your letter of the 23rd day of last month in Osaka on the 8th day of this month. With reference to the Higo barons' uprising, Ankokuji Ekei has set out as far as the Higo border and has been passing on military intelligence; so I rest satisfied.
>
> Item, you have been on your guard and have entered diligently into the matter, I have conferred with Ryūzōji Masaie about sending the troops of both Chikugo and Hizen provinces into Higo. Takakage is at present in Kurume castle, of which his brother Hidekane is the keeper, he has taken overall command with Ankokuji Ekei to assist him as his Second in Command. If it proves difficult to conquer them by means of the men of Chikugo and Hizen then invite the armies of Kuroda Kangeyu and Mori Yoshinari to gather in Kurume castle and set out together with them as a second division…
>
> Item, whatever may happen in whatever province, you are to hold fast to the principles of defence.[4]

Two later letters to Kobayakawa Takakage show that Hideyoshi's orders were being followed and that he fully appreciated the seriousness of the situation. Once again he condemns Sassa Narimasa when he writes on 9m 15d (16 October):

---

3 Oyama 1993, pp. 86–87.
4 Oyama 2003, pp. 87–89.

I have seen the report in the letter from Ankokuji Ekei and combined it with your letter of the 5th day of last month. You have gone to Kurume. The vanguard have arrived at Nankan and entered the castle, exactly as ordered. Sassa Narimasa, contrary to the instructions in my previous letter sent to him personally under my honourable vermilion seal, has transferred fiefs to the provincial samurai, and that is not good. In connection with this I have conveyed my intentions to Mōri Terumoto that he must set out for Tachibana castle. Kuroda Kangeyu, Mori Iki-no-Kami and others have also gone to Tachibana, where discussions are taking place while they await the order to advance.[5]

Three days later Hideyoshi writes again:

I received intelligence from Ankokuji Ekei on his arrival at Nankan. Trouble has quickly developed. Concerning our tactics, I have passed on my wishes to Ankokuji in a letter. Discuss them with him. Be on your guard and bring the *ikki* to justice.[6]

Kobayakawa Takakage then appears to have written a letter to Hideyoshi on 10m 6d (6 November) apprising him of the situation. Hideyoshi clearly trusted Takakage's local judgement, because he did not feel it was necessary to reply until 10m 22d (22 November), when he referred to the raid on the supply column:

I perused your letter of the 6th day of last month while in Osaka on the 22nd day of this month. I note that supplies have entered the Yūdō *tsukejiro* just as was ordered, this is good. In addition, at the time of this battle, Tachibana Sakon Shōkan Muneshige vfought fiercely and took many enemy heads. Even though this by no means the start of his military prowess, I believe that he did his very best in performing his exploits, particularly in the attack. The significance must be conveyed when you relate this specially in any letter. He must be praised to the skies.[7]

The letter continues with the first reference in Hideyoshi's correspondence to the baronial family whose castle of Tanaka would soon provide the fiercest battle of the entire Higo Rebellion:

…Wani Chikazane was not able to snatch away the supplies, but he has joined forces with Hebaru Noto-no-Kami Chikayuki and Ōtsuyama Kawachi-no-Kami Iekado to participate in the Higo Rebellion. They have assembled in Tanaka Castle with its keeper Wani Chikazane as the commander… Having heard the news of Wani Chikazane's support for the local rebellion, I have established a council of war and decided on a siege.[8]

With that simple summary Hideyoshi approved the new operation. The siege of Tanaka Castle was about to begin.

---

5 Oyama 2003, p. 89.
6 Oyama 1993, p. 90.
7 Oyama 2003, pp. 94–96.
8 Oyama 2003, pp. 94–96.

C1 Naitō Masatoyo (1522-75) epitomises the ideal of a samurai general such as the commanders who besieged Tanaka. He fought for the Takeda family and was killed at the battle of Nagashino in 1575.

C2 Samurai leaders were served by hereditary retainers. This is one of the most famous of them: Yamanaka Shika-no-Suke (1545-78), who fought to the death to preserved the Amako family.

C3 In this print a mounted samurai, who has discarded his bow for a sword, receives a spear thrust from a samurai on foot. Tanaka's *ukimusha* would have looked like the latter.

C4 This veteran barefoot warrior is the perfect image of the part-time *jizamurai* who fought against Hideyoshi in the Higo Rebellion.

C5 During a fierce battlefield melee a typical fighting samurai holds down his victim as he prepares to cut off the unfortunate man's head.

C6 The lowest ranking warriors who fought on a battlefield were the ashigaru (foot soldiers). When they were organised into disciplined weapon squads such as these musketeers at the battle of Nagakute (1584) they were very effective.

C7 This *ema* (votive picture) hangs inside the Kumano Shrine adjacent to Tanaka Castle. It shows combat commensurate with the times of the Tanaka operation. Two mounted samurai are engaged. One wields his sword; the other holds a massive iron club.

C8 An incident from the Siege of Tanaka. The scene depicted here is the first assault on Tanaka Castle. The view is from the southeast and shows the unit of the besieging army under Tachibana Muneshige attacking the area of the castle known as the Hiakeguchi. It is early morning, and the hills to the west, where Mōri Hidekane has his headquarters, are visible in the distance behind the bare skeleton of the hill of Tanaka, made more stark by a light sprinkling of snow. Its distinctive sections have been stripped of almost all their vegetation and the defences provided by their steep slopes are augmented by wooden fences and palisades. The focus of the attack is the Hiake Gate, a simple stout wooden structure with an open firing platform above. From the gate a path leads up past the Hiake Yashiki — a collection of wooden buildings — towards the main baileys of the castle, where observation towers have been erected. Gunfire erupts from the loopholes in the lower fence as the enemy army approach. They are firing over the heads of their own men, who have made a brave counter attack out of the gate, across the freezing water of the Odagawa and on to the hard surface of the rice stubble in the fields beyond. Here the two sides meet and lower their spears for a decisive clash that will produce many casualties in Hideyoshi's besieging force and cause the Odagawa to run red with blood. (Artwork by Peter Dennis © Helion & Company 2019)

6

The Wani Family and Tanaka Castle

The basis for the grievance that forced the Wani into rebellion against Hideyoshi so soon after supporting his invasion of Kyushu was the same as that expressed by the other Higo *kokujin*: that Hideyoshi's appointee Sassa Narimasa had exceeded his powers as their new overlord. On 9m 7d (7 October) the Wani family, now exposed as enemies of Narimasa because of their attack on the supply column at Hirano, ensconced themselves within Tanaka Castle and began the enhancement of its defences and the stockpiling of weapons and supplies. Their act of defiance would ultimately last one hundred days, even though a besieging army did not arrive on site to challenge them until 10m 16d (25 November).[1] Distant threats then gave way to a month-long siege that only ended because of an act of treachery. Throughout this time Tanaka stood up to Hideyoshi's army and provided a considerable threat to his authority.

The Wani of Tanaka

The Wani 和仁 family were among Higo Province's most influential barons. Their castle is variously referred to in the historical records as Tanaka Castle 田中城, Wani Castle, or Wani-Tanaka Castle, with the ideograph for *wani* sometimes being written using the single character 鰐 that otherwise means 'crocodile', although the name of its owners is never written in this way.[2] In an early reference to the place from about the year 1200 the daughter of a member of the Kurogi family is said to be married to the lord of Wani castle.[3] The site must have been in continuous occupation for the next three centuries, because in 1518 the then baron Wani Chikatsugu, named as the son of Wani Chikasada, is noted as carrying out repairs to the local Kumano Shrine. In 1521 he established the Tendai sect's Tōshōji as the Wani's *bōdaiji*

---

1   Araki 2012, pp. 203 & 74.
2   Oyama 2003, p. 162.
3   Oyama 2003, pp. 162–163.

(family temple). It was burned to the ground during the siege of 1587 and was replaced by the present Tōjōji in 1596.[4] According to *Wani Gundan*, by 1587 the Wani landownings stretched to over 120 *chō* (119 hectares) in total and straddled the border between Higo and Chikugo across a discontinuous patchwork of rice fields. In Tamana District in Higo the family owned the villages of Wani, Kichiji and Jichō, and in Yamaga District they owned Imō Village. The Wani also owned Shiragi in Chikugo Province, and an additional sourced cited by Kunitake puts their total domain as equivalent to 2,015 *koku*.[5]

Like all their fellow *kokujin* the Wani were involved in warfare with powerful neighbours, and conflict is recorded in 1340 where we read of the lord of Wani entrenching himself there during the Nambokuchō War when the dispute that pitted two rival emperors against each other spread to Kyushu.[6] Tanaka Castle was attacked as part of this campaign in 1342.[7] In 1550 the Wani were among the barons who gave support to the deposed and exiled puppet *shugo* Kikuchi Yoshitake, and along with Hebaru and Ōtsuyama they attacked the Shōdai in Tsutsugatake Castle to aid Yoshitake's efforts.[8]

The Wani must have abandoned the Kikuchi cause for the Ōtomo sometime before 1578, because in that year they attacked a Kikuchi-held castle.[9] The fifth lunar month of 1579 then saw the advance into Higo by Ryūzōji Takanobu that was supported by Kumabe Chikanaga, but the Wani stayed loyal to the Ōtomo when Tanaka Castle was attacked for the second time in its history.[10] The Ryūzōji assault was successfully driven off, so in that same year a confident Wani Chikatsugu joined forces with Ōtsuyama Sukefuyu at the battle of Shiratori on 5m 5d (30 May).[11] Little is known of the Wani's movements when the Shimazu invaded Higo following the destruction of the Ryūzōji in 1584, but they must have submitted peacefully to the Shimazu along with their fellow *kokujin*, because an entry in the diary kept by a general of the Shimazu notes that 'Lord Wani received with thanks a gift of twenty bolts of white linen'.[12]

Baron Wani Chikatsugu produced five children. The oldest was a girl who was married to Hebaru Chikayuki 辺春親行 of Sakamoto Castle, the most northerly of the Higo strongpoints, which was located on the mountainous border between Higo and Chikugo. The other four children were sons, although *Wani Gundan* mentions only three of them in connection with the siege of Tanaka. This was because Wani Chikatsugu, in a process by no means uncommon at the time, had sent his second son Munezane to be adopted by Ono Akiyuki of Miike (modern Ōmuta City, Fukuoka Prefecture). This

4   Oyama 2003, p. 164.
5   Kunitake 1993, p. 115.
6   Oyama 2003, pp. 162–163.
7   Kunitake 1993, p. 138.
8   Oyama 2003, p. 167.
9   Oyama 2003, p. 167.
10   Oyama 2003, p. 167; Kunitake 1993, p. 138
11   Araki 1987, p. 71; Oyama 2003, p. 167.
12   Various Authors, *Nihon Jōhaku Taikei Vol. 18* (1979) p. 20.

The three Wani brothers who defended Tanaka Castle so valiantly are now commemorated by these statues. From left to right they are Jinki Chikamune, who was 'more bear than man', Kageyu Chikazane, the Commander of Tanaka, and the immensely strong Danjō Chikanori. Behind them is the Tanaka Castle site, seen from a very similar angle to the drawing on the Tanaka map.

would ensure that if the family were wiped out someone would survive to carry on the blood line, as did indeed happen at Tanaka. Wani Munezane became Ono Kyūemon Munezane, and when Tanaka fell he was able to provide a place of refuge for his pregnant sister-in-law.[13]

Wani Chikatsugu died some time before the Higo Rebellion began, so the defence of Tanaka Castle fell on the shoulders of the new head of the family: his heir Wani Kageyu Chikazane 和仁勘解由親実. He was ably assisted by two younger brothers. The first was called Wani Danjō Chikanori 和仁弾正親範, who is described as a giant of a man and 'strong enough to lift a three-legged iron cauldron'. The younger Wani Jinki Chikamune 和仁人鬼親宗 was equally impressive, being red faced and very hairy, 'more bear than man', so that his name Jinki could appropriately be written using the two characters 人鬼 that mean 'man-devil'.[14] Together with a handful of loyal retainers they awaited the arrival of Hideyoshi's army.

13   Oyama 2003, p. 165.
14   Kumamoto 2000, p.63

The *okajiro* of Tanaka

The site of Tanaka Castle nowadays is a distinctive and isolated hill in a beautiful and largely unspoiled rural area in the northern part of Kumamoto Prefecture known as Nagomi Town. Nagomi was formed in 2006 by the merger of the former towns of Mikawa and Kikusui, hence the references to both Mikawa and Nagomi as places of publication for the modern printed sources. The tranquil mountains around the castle site are densely forested; the rice fields are terraced and in summer fireflies can be enjoyed beside its streams and rivers. It is a peaceful spot partly because the modern Kyushu Expressway runs five kilometres to the west and keeps through traffic away from its secluded valley, out of which a minor road makes its way along hairpin bends to enter Fukuoka Prefecture over the Yabetani Pass.

From the air the Tanaka castle hill has the appearance of a tongue-shaped series of terraces projecting sharply in a southerly direction, although the first thing that catches the attention of a visitor is how small the overall site is compared to the tall wooded mountains that tower around it. The hill's highest point is only 104 metres above sea level and stands a mere 60 metres above the flat river valley at its foot. In winter the outline of Tanaka's compact mound is particularly stark and rugged, showing how it provided protection for the Wani family in 1587 by acting as the bony skeleton of a typical medieval Japanese castle.

The name most frequently used to describe this style of fortress is *yamashiro* 山城 (mountain castle). A *yamashiro* was a stockaded wooden structure with towers, fences, palisades, gates and buildings set upon and among the natural contours of a mountain, although considerable efforts were made to adapt and enhance those contours by using man-made ditches, ramparts and levelled terraces. A *yamashiro* was therefore carved as much as it was built, with the area being stripped and shaped to convert it to the best defensive purposes. Skilful digging (done very carefully to avoid the risk of erosion and weather damage) and a limited use of undressed stone added walls and dry moats around the perimeter and in between various sections within the castle. These would often cover a huge area, with the uppermost point affording extensive views.

Several words other than *yamashiro* are used to describe medieval castles more precisely according to their size, status, location and elevation, and as the hill of Tanaka is of modest proportions the expression *okajiro* 丘城 (hilltop castle) would be an appropriate one for the fortress built upon it.[15] Tanaka nevertheless consisted of a carved and strengthened structure similar to the larger *yamashiro*, but we must banish from our minds any idea that these medieval strongpoints were spectacular white-walled Japanese castles like the seventeenth century examples at Himeji or Hikone, with their golden decorations, tiled roofs and elegant plastered walls. Those places, which soar above huge stone bases made by cladding the existing hillsides in massive shaped stone blocks, were designed to intimidate rivals by combining the

---

15   For a useful list see <http://www.lint.ne.jp/~uematsu/yogokaisetu.html> (Accessed 15 August 2018).

strength of a fortress with the grandeur of a lavish mansion, displaying reception rooms and exquisite gardens. By contrast Tanaka Castle, like most *yamashiro*, was a purely military installation that was not designed for permanent residential use other than by a rotating garrison. The Wani family and their senior retainers would have lived in some state in manors round about that ranged from grand mansions to large farmhouses according to the owners' rank and wealth. These places would be abandoned in wartime for the security of the castle, where extra dwellings would be rapidly constructed to accommodate a greatly increased population.

In 1587 Tanaka Castle would have appeared from afar as a complex wooden structure with numerous fenced terraces topped by open towers. It was literally built upon a rock, because the hill of Tanaka is the result of an ancient eruption of Mount Aso, and several small caves can be found around its perimeter. That gift of nature gave Tanaka's designers an advantage over most other *yamashiro* builders, because Tanaka's shape was partly carved from soft stone which may have been enhanced by some dressed stone walls, although no trace remains of any. Tanaka's rocky outcrop is particularly noticeable nowadays at its extremities. For example, the north-western corner of the site is an exposed cliff face known as Iwa Jizō 岩地蔵, so called because relief carvings of the deity Jizō were added to it in the year 1471.[16] These natural features provided a defensible position, gave an excellent

The hill of Tanaka Castle is shown here in its stark winter outline from the north-east. Its volcanic origins are indicated by the two small caves. In the foreground we see the northern demaru around which passes the modern approach road. Behind it, and obscured by the grove of bamboo, is the higher ni no maru. The white crash barrier marks the present-day course of the Oda River, which acted as Tanaka's eastern moat. This is the view that would have been seen by the besiegers serving under Chikushi Hirokado.

---

16 This part of the castle suffered minor damage during the January 2019 earthquake that struck the immediate area.

viewpoint and defied attackers from the strong palisades and steep slopes that were artificially created upon them. Most importantly, all these elements could be quickly enhanced and strengthened when danger threatened, as it did in 1587.

The overall layout of Tanaka castle is briefly summarised in Volume 18 of *Nihon Jōhaku Taikei,* (Japanese castles in outline).[17] Its short description of Tanaka is based on the results of the archaeological investigation of the site that were dramatically confirmed by the battle map, which was discovered in 1989 when a local scholar decided to look for material relating to the Tanaka campaign in the extensive archives of the Mōri family. The search was undertaken because the Mōri were well represented at the siege and one of their number, Mōri Hidekane, was in overall command. The remarkable document that came to light bears the title *Hebaru-Wani shiyori jindori zu,* (plan of the layout of the battle formation for the attack on the Hebaru and the Wani).[18] It is Japan's oldest surviving battle map, and includes a drawing of the castle and a schematic plan of the attackers' siege lines, together with some fascinating written orders for the army's conduct during the siege.[19]

The most noticeable feature of the Tanaka battle map is a drawing of the castle done as a side elevation, which matches up remarkably to the results of the dig. The castle is depicted within the double palisade built by Hideyoshi's army during the siege, and the picture is roughly the view that would have been obtained from the besieging commander's headquarters across the river. It is orientated from north to south along a horizontal axis, although the northern section of the defences is shown upside down for clarity. It contains various symbols and there are a few added notes. The picture confirms the castle's *okajiro* style, because it reveals a distinctively shaped hill consisting of several typical separate and artificially levelled terraces known as *kuruwa* 曲 輪 that are linked by twisted footpaths shown as curving lines.

Both the picture and the excavations reveal that the site of Tanaka Castle consists of three separate layers of *kuruwa*, each divided from the one above it by steep and almost inaccessible banks that extend around most of the site. Some of these vertiginous slopes are themselves terraced in tight successive stages like gigantic steps, the most pronounced examples of which lie on the northern side of the hill where there is a small shrine to the deity Bishamon-ten. The innermost area of Tanaka is the highest point of the castle, where any peak that ever existed has long been levelled to make two flat *kuruwa*. The higher and smaller of the two follows convention by being called the *honmaru*本丸 (the 'inner bailey' to use a European analogy). According to the drawing on the map it had a fence around it and included a high wooden openwork *yagura*櫓 (lookout tower). Numerous postholes indicate a high density of building. The much larger *kuruwa* just a few metres below is called

---

17 Various Authors *Nihon Jōhaku Taikei Vol. 18* (Tokyo: Shinjimbutsu, 1979), pp. 184–186.

18 It is item 892 in the catalogue of the Mōri family collection in Yamaguchi Prefectural Archives.

19 In 1990 a special symposium was organised where the progress and significance of the excavation was discussed and related to the revelations arising from its data. In 1999 materials from the 1990 symposium and later research were published in a separate volume that directly related the map to the physical layout of the site. This work (Mikawa 1999) has provided most of the information which follows that is based on the map.

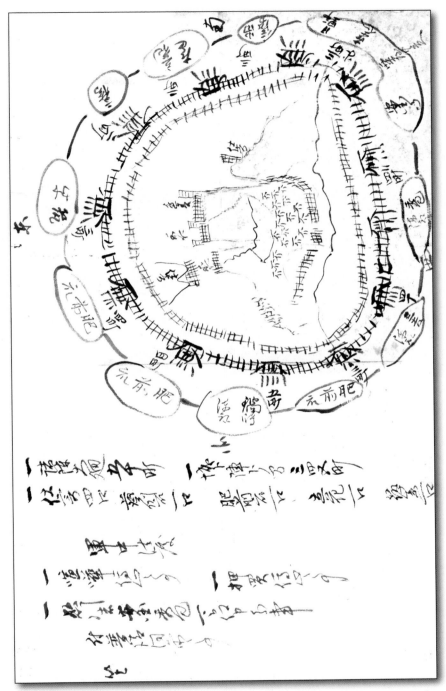

The Tanaka battle map, discovered by chance in the archives of the Mōri family. On the left are the various items of written information discussed in the text. The series of cartouches identify the besieging commanders and indicate their distances away from the castle. The two-layered outer fence was erected as part of the siege operation. The most interesting section lies within this fence, and is a view of Tanaka Castle from the west. The honmaru and ni no maru are shown at slightly different elevations and are surrounded by fences with three towers. The V- shaped ditch divides off the western demaru. The southern demaru is shown in dramatic separation from the main castle and the defenders' fence appeared to run inside it. The northern demaru is depicted upside down. Also shown are the barracks and the line of the Wani River.

This photograph shows the dramatic outline of the western demaru and the ni-no-maru, which matches up exactly with the drawing on the Tanaka battle map.

the *ni no maru* 二の丸 ('second bailey'). Again it is shown on the map with a protective fence and what are likely to be two towers. The wide *ni no maru* is now accessed by a steep and narrow modern road that winds round the castle hill from the north-east to a small car park in the *ni no maru*. The overall area of the combined *honmaru* and *ni no maru* is roughly heart-shaped, measuring about 150 metres north to south and 100 metres east to west.

As shown on the diagram on page 57, below the inner defensive core formed by these two central *maru* lies a layer of three other smaller but very distinctive *kuruwa*. Each is completely isolated from the innermost area because the castle hill has been sliced through just below the *ni no maru* by a five metre-deep steep-sided ditch that runs around three-quarters of the site except for the south-west, where the slope of the hill is already very pronounced owing to the natural cliff. When added to the dimensions of the inner core the combined *kuruwa* cover a total overall defensive area of 600 metres north to south and 400 metres east to west as measured at its widest points. Kunitake quotes some historical dimensions found in the archives of the Ono family that correspond very closely to these figures, which are based on the results of the archaeological excavation.[20]

The three isolated spurs created by the ditch are known as *demaru* 出丸 (detached baileys), although the southern spur is also referred to as the *san*

---

20 Kunitake 1993, p. 115.

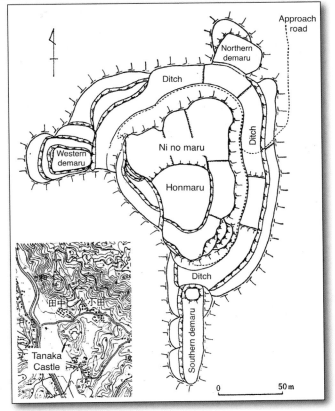

This very steep succession of short terraces lies on the north side of Tanaka below the ni-no-maru. A small Buddhist graveyard occupies one level nowadays.

A plan of the inner defences of Tanaka Castle, from Volume 18 of Nihon Jōhaku Taikei.

This picture is taken looking down from the eastern side of the ni no maru to the dry ditch that was cut around the castle inner area to create three separated sectors known as demaru.

*no maru*三の丸 (third bailey). This one is long and narrow and is separated from the *ni no maru* by an extremely wide gap, leaving very steep slopes on each side of the ditch. Post holes and a very clear depiction on the drawing reveal that there was a wooden tower on it during the siege of 1587, but there is no indication on the picture of a bridge across to the *ni no maru*, which would have been a vital necessity for the isolated defenders and probably resembled the one reconstructed at Uto Castle. The *san no maru* was one of the sites chosen by Mōri Hidekane for the final attack and would have seen some very fierce fighting.

On the northern side of the castle the ditch has separated the *ni no maru* from the largest of the three isolated *demaru*. In the account of the fighting in *Wani Gundan* this spur is called Miyatake 宮嶽 and covered the main entrance to the castle through its northern gate. Because it has the same name as the large mountain just outside Tanaka the author of *Wani Gundan* refers to it as 'Miyatake inside the castle'. It is a formidable part of the Tanaka site; its steep terraced face dominates the view of the castle from the north-east and almost obscures any sight of the larger and higher *ni no maru* behind it. In the picture on the map the hill of Miyatake is depicted upside down to avoid it being obscured by the drawing of the western *demaru*.

On the drawing this smaller western *demaru* – a prominent feature of the castle nowadays when seen from the main car park below – is divided from the inner baileys by a ditch that seems artistically exaggerated, but the excavation has revealed that the *demaru* was indeed separated from the *ni no maru* by a dramatic V-shaped cutting. Post holes show also that the

The simple reconstructed wooden bridge at Uto Castle. The bridges connecting the various sections of Tanaka would probably have looked very much like this one.

western *demaru* was completely enclosed by a fence as on the drawing. It has very steep sides on its outer faces, and Kunitake has suggested that two further post holes on the *ni no maru* were supports for a drawbridge across to it. The bridge platform could be raised or lowered at will by means of rope and pulleys.[21] The western *demaru* is known today as the Nishisute guruwa 西捨て曲輪 ('western abandoned *kuruwa*'), suggesting that it was either evacuated or lost to the enemy at some stage during the siege.[22]

The shapes of the western and southern *demaru* make them somewhat reminiscent of a development current at the time in European military architecture, which was the creation of the ravelin: a detached angle bastion. The angle bastion, a projecting tower often of pentagonal shape, regarded by one authority on military architecture as 'the most radically effective architectural element since the arch', replaced the round or square towers of medieval castles because its straight sides and broad angles allowed no blind spots for an attacker to exploit.[23] Although enormously expensive to build in stone these mathematically designed terraces began to appear throughout Europe, and in some wealthier communities the trend resulted in a city wall that was a perfectly symmetrical multi-pointed star. In the Netherlands they were created from earth rather than

21 Kunitake 1993, pp. 156–157.
22 Kunitake 1993, pp. 155–156.
23 Hale, J.R. 'The Early Development of the Bastion: An Italian Chronology *c.*1450–1534' in J.R. Hale (ed.), *Renaissance War Studies* (London: A.C. Black, 1983), p. 2.

A view of the western demaru (detached bailey) looking down from the terrace of the ni-no-maru. During the siege it was probably connected to the ni-no-maru by means of a bridge, possibly a drawbridge.

stone, making them look much like a Japanese *yamashiro*. A ravelin – the detached version of a bastion – was entirely separated from the castle or city walls that it protected. This allowed additional defensive fire to be directed against any attackers who had entered the ditch between it and the main sectors of the castle.

The Japanese-style ravelins of Tanaka would have allowed the Wani many of the advantages of the more complex European model, and the way in which they have been deliberately shaped suggests precisely such an intention. While they were still being held by the garrison a wide field of fire could have been delivered from them during an attack. Covering shots from the inner baileys above would be made to follow the lines of their edges to keep any climbers at bay, sweeping them off the slopes without risking their own men inside the defences. Conversely, if a ravelin was lost to an enemy, concentrated fire could be poured into it from the castle above.

The drawing on the map suggests that these two layers of terraces were the key defensive areas of the castle, but other *kuruwa* existed further down the hill and are shown together with certain modern features of the site on page 61. These places combined defensive purposes with domestic ones and could be abandoned in the face of an attack. To the south-west, below a very steep slope down from the *ni no maru,* is a terrace called the Shinshiro 新 城 (new castle). On the map it corresponds to an area bearing a number of symbols in the shape of the Greek letter *pi*. It has been concluded that these indicate the barracks for the soldiers, because an identical symbol appears on a later battle plan for the siege of Odawara in 1590 that is also owned

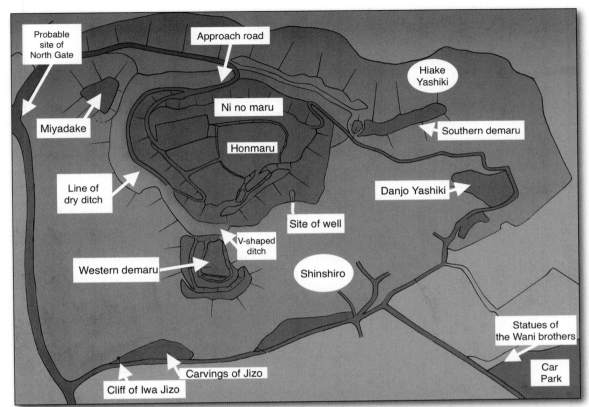

Probable
site of
North Gate

Approach road

Hiake
Yashiki

Miyadake

Ni no maru

Honmaru

Southern demaru

Line of
dry ditch

Danjo Yashiki

Site of well

V-shaped
ditch

Shinshiro

Western demaru

Statues of
the Wani brothers

Car
Park

Carvings of Jizo

Cliff of Iwa Jizo

A plan of the present day site of Tanaka Castle. Note how the dry ditch cuts off the three detached demaru from the inner area. Below them are the three lower kuruwa (terraces) known as the Shinshiro, the Hiake Yashiki and the Danjō Yashiki.

by Yamaguchi Prefectural Archives.[24] There are 18 barracks symbols in all on the map, a number consistent with the figure suggested by the postholes uncovered during excavation.

A smaller flat area adjacent to the Shinshiro has been identified as the site of the castle's well, while to the south and at approximately the same elevation of the Shinshiro lies a large terrace known as the Danjō Yashiki 弾正屋敷, so called because it is identified locally as the site of Wani Danjō's *yashiki* or mansion. Post holes have been discovered that suggest the existence of an appropriately sized structure within the overall area of the terrace. A similar *kuruwa* across the hill to the east is called the Hiake Yashiki 日明屋敷 and probably also contained domestic buildings that could be abandoned during an attack for the safety of the inner areas. The Hiake Yashiki was the target of one of the first attacks on Tanaka.

The outermost natural defensive layer of Tanaka Castle on its western side was provided by the Wanigawa 和仁川 (Wani River), which is shown on the drawing as a wavy line. Another river – the Odagawa 小田川 – flows on the eastern side of the castle.[25] The course of both rivers has changed greatly over the centuries, and their flows were channelled and culverted about 30 years ago to make them into little more than streams, but the course of

---

24 Reproduced in Mikawa 1999, p. 58.
25 Kunitake 1993, p. 113.

the Wanigawa in 1587 has been identified because of the swampy ground and the existence of pebbles and rocks associated with an old river bed. It was much wider and deeper then and ran right up to the castle below the Shinshiro, so one can envisage its waters raging against the rocks of the Iwa Jizō to provide a formidable barrier to any attacker. Nowadays the controlled Odagawa flows precisely along the eastern defences of Tanaka as a watery cordon. It too would have been much more extensive in 1587, surging round the almost vertical cliff at the castle's southern tip.

The Built Structures of Tanaka

As to the nature of the structures raised on top of these shaped areas, no buildings are shown on the map and none of the main gateways, towers, bridges or domestic buildings of Tanaka has ever been rebuilt, so their probable shape has to be inferred from the post holes, from drawings on the map or by comparison with certain careful reconstructions of contemporary castles made elsewhere in Japan. The rebuilt Arato Castle in Nagano Prefecture is the most helpful. It is situated at a much higher elevation than Tanaka, but the overall defensive area is much the same and includes buildings and fences reconstructed in an appropriate style.

At the time of the siege both the *honmaru* and *ni no maru* would have contained many important wooden buildings for domestic, administrative and storage purposes, and nowadays ornamental bushes mark the sites of the post holes located within the *honmaru*. Not much rice was found during the excavation of Tanaka so there can have been no massive stockpiles inside big warehouses as there were in some castles, neither are there any post holes to suggest such large buildings. Nor too is there any outline of a multi-storeyed building on the drawing, so there is unlikely to have been a 'keep' of any sort. In all likelihood the buildings at Tanaka were simple one-storey wooden constructions with sloping roofs very much like the reconstructed examples at Arato with their tightly shuttered doors and overhanging eaves. There is no archaeological evidence for tiled roofs at Tanaka, so the builders must have used either thatch or wooden shingles as at Arato, weighted down using rows of heavy stones.

Four openwork observation towers are depicted in some detail in the drawing, although their lower sections are partly obscured by the sketches of the fences. These illustrations shows that Tanaka had one tower in the *honmaru* built from five- or six-storey sections of timber and two lower towers of two storeys fewer. A fourth *yagura* is shown completely isolated on the southern *demaru*. Judging by these sketches, none of Tanaka's towers had roofs, and a useful reconstruction may be seen at a samurai theme park in Ise called the Azuchi-Momoyama Bunka Mura. The *yagura* on each side of the main entrance at Ise are just like the ones on the Tanaka drawing, although their defences have been augmented using portable wooden shields: a sensible addition that was probably used when Tanaka's defences were enhanced.

The inner defences of Arato Castle include one-storeyed buildings, simple fences and gateways. The domestic and adminstrative buildings are of wooden construction with shuttered windows. They are roofed with wooden shingles, held in place by rows of stones. Tanaka would have looked much like this.

This reconstruction of an openwork wooden tower is actually at the entrance to a theme park, but it matches up exactly to the pictures of similar structures that are shown on the Tanaka battle map. The portable wooden shields add to the defences.

The bridges that connected Tanaka's *demaru* to the inner defences would also have been very simple, and the example rebuilt at Uto Castle is likely to reflect the Tanaka design. It has one central support arising from the ditch below. An alternative unsupported design has been reconstructed at Hachigata Castle, where there are also simple fences similar in construction to the ones sketched on the Tanaka map. The larger double fence on the map was built by the besiegers and will be discussed later.

The longer of the inner fences makes up Tanaka's outer man-made defence line on its western side. It encircles the barracks area of the Shinshiro and has two prominent gaps that suggest gateways. Presumably the fence extended right round the site apart from these gaps, although on the drawing it terminates abruptly on the northern side where the hill is shown falling away sharply below the western *demaru* and a series of scratch-like marks are drawn on the edge of the hillside. These pictorial features probably indicate the natural defences on this side of the castle: the cliff of Iwa Jizō and the very steep slopes of the hill beyond. Both would have been very difficult to climb, making the addition of an outer fence unnecessary. The fence must have recommenced on the other side of Miyatake as an outer defence line, integrated into whatever structure made up the northern gateway. The most interesting feature of the fence, however, lies on its southern side, because instead of encircling the southern *demaru* it passes through the ditch between it and the *ni no maru*, along the line of a path that still exists. The southern *demaru* is therefore isolated from the inner defences, and only a bridge could have saved its defenders if the sector was lost.

In addition to this outer fence two inner fences encircle the *honmaru* and *ni no maru*. Just like the outer fence they are depicted pictorially as a series of sharpened wooden stakes linked together using some form of horizontal connection. This may well be a completely accurate depiction, because alternative designs known elsewhere were never much more elaborate. The inner fences at Hachigata, Arato and Uto have been reconstructed in a similar way, and on top of Tanaka's *honmaru* nowadays there is a modern fence rebuilt in exactly this style. However, these openwork fences would have provided poor protection for the areas of the castle that were likely to come under direct fire, so a more likely style for the fences outside the inner baileys would have used vertical posts or planks fitted tightly together with loopholes cut through them, or even some form of plastered wall as shown on the contemporary screen of the battle of Nagashino depicted on page 65.

The Nagashino screen also shows a gateway, and one key to understanding the siege of Tanaka lies in visualising the structure and layout of its entry points. They feature prominently in the discussions of the fighting in *Wani Gundan*, where three entrances are identified. The gateway on the northern side is referred to in the literature as the Kitanoguchi 北の口 (northern approach). Any North Gate that may have existed gave access to the fortifications somewhere around a prominent spur below the northern *demaru* above a lower ditch, although the modern road has removed any traces of it. An approach on the south-eastern side is referred to as the Hiakeguchi 日明口 and probably entered the castle via the terrace of the

This modern copy in Nakatsu Castle of the famous painted screen of the battle of Nagashino shows a type of gateway and a stronger version of a wall that may have existed at Tanaka. The wall is of rough plaster on top of a wood and lath framework and is pierced with loopholes. The thatch on top protects the plaster from rain. This design would have afforded much better protection than the openwork stake fences.

This reconstructed section of Uto Castle shows a small covered gate and an openwork fence of sharpened stakes such as is depicted on the Tanaka battle map.

Hiake Yashiki. There is also no sign of it nowadays, nor of the Shinshiroguchi 新城口, which must have been an entrance through the outer defence works of the Shinshiro. An Ōteguchi 大手口 (main gateway) may have followed a vague path up the steep northern terraces to enter the *honmaru*, although the name probably refers only to the main entrance of the *honmaru* and not an outer entrance, because it lies on the same side of the castle as the Kitanoguchi. It was therefore probably just a continuation of the northern entrance.

The gate of the honmaru is the only entrance at Tanaka to have been rebuilt, and is very similar to other simple gateways seen on contemporary illustrations.

As to the structure of these gateways, the entrance to Tanaka's *honmaru* has been rebuilt as a stout but simple design of two uprights topped with a crossbeam, and an authentic contemporary illustration of several similar gates with small roofs may be seen on a painted screen depicting Hideyoshi's Hizen-Nagoya Castle. As Hizen-Nagoya was constructed to be the base for assembling Hideyoshi's expeditionary force for the invasion of Korea in 1592 there was no anticipation of any attack. Rudimentary entrances were therefore sufficient, and ones similar to them have been reconstructed all over Japan to mark the innermost sectors of defended fortresses. The outer gateways, however, must have been stronger if they were to withstand attack and were possibly reinforced with blocks of undressed stone, with walls or fences on either side that were overlooked by, and easily defensible from the hillside above. The Shinshiroguchi in particular would have required a solid gateway because the overall slope of the castle hill is gentler on this side than any other.

The Nagashino screen shows a solid one-storey gatehouse integrated into a solid wall with no additional features, but when it came to defending a gateway the simplest model of all was of two storeys with an open firing platform built above it. An excellent reconstruction has been made at Arato, where it encloses two heavy gates. Tanaka's entrances could well have looked like this, apart from the fact that Arato's gate is enclosed by walls made completely from stone. More elaborate varieties had enclosed upper storeys like the ones rebuilt at Torigoe Castle in Ishikawa Prefecture. Like Tanaka, Torigoe was a fortress defended by an army of lower class warriors who defied

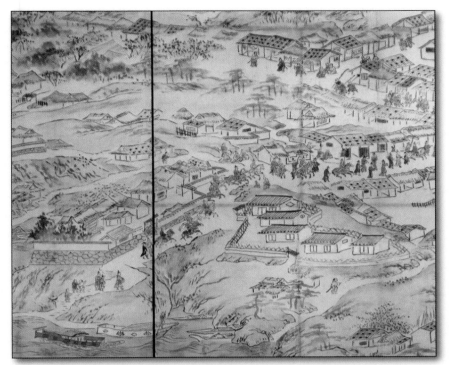

This painted screen of Hizen-Nagoya Castle, the fortress built by Hideyoshi for the invasion of Korea in 1592, shows several contemporary features that were almost certainly present at Tanaka. In the left foreground, inside shaped stone walls that were not built at Tanaka, can be seen a collection of simple one-storey buildings with thatched or shingled roofs held down by rows of heavy stones. A similar cluster appears to the right inside weaker fortifications. The inner gates are rudimentary affairs because Hizen-Nagoya was not expecting any hostile attack.

The reconstructed site of Arato Castle in Nagano Prefecture includes the simplest model of a two-storey non-enclosed fortified gateway with a firing platform on top of the gates.

a *daimyō*, and it too was overcome and burned to the ground. The larger of Torigoe's pair of two-storey gatehouses has a square plan and uses four large-diameter timbers as the vertical supports. The solid wooden gates swing back on hinges underneath a guard tower that is open at the rear but has narrow window slits at the front. There is a low balustrade running round it and the whole edifice has a sloping wooden roof. The other type of gatehouse is fully enclosed with two small postern gates. Both gateways are integrated into the surrounding earth mound, as they would have been at Tanaka.

In 1587 all of Tanaka's existing buildings, ditches and fences would have been augmented by additional ones when the siege preparations were undertaken, resulting in a tightly packed wooden complex resembling a small village inside the confines of the different *kuruwa*. Outside these areas ditches would have been cleared, trees would have been cut down and the footpaths strengthened. All these features – both natural and man made – would have been enhanced, linked and integrated using ingenuity and a lot of hard work to transform a simple carved hillside into a formidable *okajiro*. This is what happened at Tanaka in 1587, where the Japanese mountain castle model would be tested to destruction.

The Army Dispositions Inside the Castle

The total forces defending Tanaka Castle lay at something over 900 men, who were outnumbered by the attackers at a ratio of about 10 to one.[26] The garrison's positions are not shown on the Tanaka battle map, where the only suggestion of their presence are the names 'Hebaru' written above the *honmaru* and 'Wani' written above the *ni no maru* and the western *demaru*. For any further information about the army's defensive layout we must turn to *Wani Gundan*, where the locations of the defenders are listed according to the names of their commanders.

In this list the *honmaru*, somewhat surprisingly, is commanded not by Wani Chikazane but by his brother-in-law Hebaru Chikayuki. Chikazane is instead in charge of the *ni no maru* where we find also the family's loyal retainer Kusano Hayato, who is described as the captain of the *ukimusha*. Miyao believes that the *ukimusha* were used as a back-up force at Tanaka and were stationed in the broad and accessible *ni no maru* so that they could be sent anywhere in the castle with ease.[27] The other three dispositions are identified according to the entrances that they covered. The middle brother Wani Danjō and the senior retainer Matsuo Hyūga are in charge of the Hiakeguchi on the eastern side. The youngest brother Wani Jinki, together with Matsuo Ichinokami (the son of Matsuo Hyūga), cover the Kitanoguchi from Miyadake. Finally, Nakamura Jibushōyū is stationed at the Shinshiroguchi. No names are given for anyone stationed in the western *demaru*, even though 'Wani' is written above it on the map, or for the

---

26 Kunitake 1993, p. 117.
27 Miyao, Yoichi (ed.), *Nankan Kibun* (Nankan City: Nankan Board of Education, 2010), p. 43.

southern *demaru*. *Wani Gundan* gives the numbers of troops serving at each place as follows:

Honmaru	Over 300 men	100 muskets, 80 bows, 50 spears
Ni no maru	Over 100 men	30 muskets, 20 bows, 30 spears
(plus *ukimusha*	Over 100 men	20 muskets, 30 bows, 30 spears)
Hiakeguchi	Over 150 men	30 muskets, 30 bows
Kitanoguchi	Over 100 men	20 muskets, 20 bows
Shinshiroguchi	Over 150 men	30 muskets, 30 bows, 20 spears[28]

The separate mention of muskets, bows and spears is unlikely to refer only to the numbers of these weapons, but also to the soldiers who had been trained to use them, of which the musketeers and archers would be skilled missile troops. The spears would have been wielded by low-ranking samurai, and the situation of defending a castle explains the concentration on firepower rather than spear points. The balance of the given numbers for each contingent would have been made up by the more heavily armoured men who used personal edged weapons: the warriors conventionally known as samurai. So the 'over 150 men' listed under the command of Nakamura Jibushōyū at the Shinshiroguchi, for example, would be a force of 70 samurai together with 30 musketeers, 30 archers and 20 spearmen.

As has been noted earlier, the distinction between samurai and supposedly lower class warriors was a very vague one throughout Japan at this time, and this was particularly so among the *jizamurai* and *ukimusha* of the Higo barons. The majority of the *bushi* at Tanaka would therefore have been *jizamurai*. They were not a social élite apart from the family members and their closest hereditary retainers, some of whom would have owned and ridden horses, although horses would have been of limited use in the siege situation. These mounted men would be accompanied by personal attendants. In other historical records the numbers of horsemen in an army is given in units of *ki*, which means a fighting unit consisting of a samurai and his immediate followers such as grooms and weapon carriers, their number depending upon the owner's rank and personal wealth. Allowing for the presence of such men the total number of combatants within Tanaka castle would certainly have brought the figures to over 900, with the attendants making the numbers up to about 1,000.

The *jizamurai* may not have been a social élite, but their behaviour at Tanaka certainly portrays them as a military élite, whose weapons would have been some form of pole-arm such as a *yari* (spear), a *naginata* (glaive) or a *nodachi* (long sword) in addition to the *katana* (sword) and *tantō* (dagger) worn at their belts. Some may have used muskets, although only as individual weapons that were handed to attendants for reloading, rather than as members of firearms squads. All these weapons inflicted nasty wounds from which a well-designed suit of armour afforded a considerable degree of protection, hence the popular image from woodblock prints of the

---

28 Araki (2012), pp. 56–58.

dying samurai standing firm in spite of a host of arrows protruding from him. Arrows, and to a lesser extent bullets, were however delivered from a distance, while stones dropped from a castle wall could cause quite serious injuries.

In hand-to-hand combat – the ideal to which every samurai aspired as distinct from being felled by the anonymous missile of a social inferior – spears and swords came into their own, but even then both the suits of armour and the samurai themselves showed a remarkable capacity for withstanding punishment. This resilience is dramatically illustrated by the life of a warrior whose long career was indirectly related to the events at Tanaka. He was Ono Shigeyuki (1546–1609), who acquired a younger brother when Wani Munezane was sent for adoption to continue the Wani bloodline. The record of Shigeyuki's service as a retainer of the Tachibana notes that he fought in 22 major battles including Ulsan and Sekigahara, together with over 40 minor skirmishes. During those actions he sustained wounds in 67 places on his body: five from bullets, seven from arrows and no less than 55 from sword strokes, one of which completely removed his right arm. In spite of this Shigeyuki lived to the ripe old age of 63 and died 'with his boots off'.[29]

The *Wani Gundan* figures give no indication of the numbers of non-combatants who sought refuge inside Tanaka Castle, but in view of its desperate situation the distinction between combatant and non-combatant would have been almost meaningless except in the case of the elderly, the very young and the infirm. Anyone who could fight did fight, and the option of leaving the latter in their villages or having them flee to the hills would have presented Hideyoshi's army with an unnecessary opportunity to acquire hostages. As noted earlier, there were 7,000 women and children

A samurai charges into battle against a hail of arrows. A well-designed suit of armour afforded remarkable protection against arrows delivered from a distance, hence the reference to Ono Shigeyuki sustaining multiple arrow wounds over the course of his long career.

29 The original data are included in a manuscript genealogy of the Tachibana retainers, and were kindly supplied to the author as a resume from the Miike Historical Society (Miike Historical Society *Ono-ke no keifu* (Omuta, 2017).

inside Jōmura castle.[30] The fate of the wives and children belonging to the Wani brothers is described in the narratives of the Tanaka action, so it is reasonable to assume that the other soldiers defending Tanaka had their families with them too, a conclusion strongly suggested by a letter sent immediately after the fall of the castle referring to 'no survivors: men or women'.[31] Judging by accounts of other sieges the presence of women and children in a castle would not have provoked resentment at having more mouths to feed, because they would have made themselves very useful by tending the wounded, casting bullets and preparing food. Women may even have fought beside their menfolk when necessity demanded, and such actions are well-attested, particularly in the case of *ikki* armies under siege.[32] Thus prepared, the army of the Wani barons and their desperate supporters began a act of defiance against Toyotomi Hideyoshi and his representative Sassa Narimasa that would last for one hundred days.

---

30 Mikawa 1997, p. 210; Araki 2012, p. 57.

31 Mikawa 1997, pp. 206–207 & 314–315.

32 For a well-known example see Chamberlain, Basil Hall, 'A Short Memoir from the Seventeenth Century. "Mistress An's narrative"', *Transactions of the Asiatic Society of Japan* 15 (1887), pp. 37–40.

7

The Tanaka Battle Map and the Siege Lines

After a month of preparation and anticipation on the part of the defenders, Mōri Hidekane's army arrived to take up their positions outside Tanaka on 10m 16d (25 November 1587), and it is at this point in the discussion that the Tanaka battle map makes its most valuable contribution to the study in the form of unique information that is missing from larger and better-known campaigns. As will be discussed below, neither Hideyoshi's correspondence nor the chronicles provide any information about the siege layout beyond a vague list of local place names where the besiegers were stationed. The map has radically transformed our understanding both of these locations and of the circumstances surrounding the army's deployment.

Because of its detailed description of the army's positions the Tanaka battle map acts as a highly sophisticated version of a document known in Japan as a *jindatesho*, a representation in a visual form of troops deployed for battle, of which several examples have survived. Matthew Stavros has studied the topic of *jindatesho* in detail and regards them as evidence that a military revolution was taking place in sixteenth century Japan.[1] The example Stavros illustrates in his article is the earliest known surviving *jindatesho*. It dates from 1584 and shows the deployment of Hideyoshi's armies against Tokugawa Ieyasu's Komaki Castle, although Stavros makes the mistake of concluding that it is a map of the battle of Nagakute. Nagakute took place a few days later as a result of a raid launched on Mikawa province by Hideyoshi's generals who took advantage of the fact that many of Ieyasu's troops were similarly arrayed against Hideyoshi. The battle of Nagakute was fought over a very wide area and was characterised by surprise and confusion on both sides, making it most unlikely that any of the commanders involved had the time to draw up a detailed battle plan.[2] The Komaki *jindatesho* has a more strategic purpose, and only consists of a number of names next to simple lines that show their formations and relative positions relative to Komaki Castle.

---

1   Stavros, Matthew, 'Military Revolution in Early Modern Japan' *Japanese Studies* 33, 2013, pp. 243–261.

2   Stavros 2013, pp. 255–257.

The Tanaka battle map is of a far more complex design and contains an enormous amount of information. The data include the names of the besieging commanders, a schematic plan of their dispositions in the siege lines, the highly detailed sketch of the castle's defences described above, and written information covering essential matters of army discipline. All these add greatly to our understanding of the overall strategy by which the action was approached. Other elements provide a fascinating insight into the tactics that were being put into operation at the particular moment during the siege when the map was drawn. The Tanaka document therefore has a much more dynamic nature than the Komaki diagram.

The Tanaka Siege Lines and the Besieging Commanders

Just outside the picture of the castle on the battle map lie two roughly circular drawings that clearly indicate fences. The outer one is much sturdier than the inner one. They were erected by the attacking force when the decision was made to blockade the castle after the initial assaults had failed. Their significance will be discussed later, because another broadly circular line shows where the besiegers were located when the army first arrived outside Tanaka. This line is drawn around the whole of the sketch of the castle just outside the double fence. It is purely diagrammatic and consists of a number of linked cartouches bearing the names of the besieging generals. Additional comments on the map allow us to work out the rough locations of their troops, because just outside the cartouches are written the distances from the castle where their units were stationed expressed in multiples of one *chō* (109 metres). When this information is combined with the geographical names of the camps of the besieging units that appear in *Wani Gundan* and *Wani no jō rakujō no oboe* it is possible to project on to a modern map a likely impression of the physical layout of the besieging army when it took up position surrounding Tanaka.

Turning first to the names, the question of identifying the besieging commanders is by no means straightforward, because until the discovery of the map the only information available about them was from Hideyoshi's letters and the two chronicles. *Wani Gundan* merely states that Sassa Narimasa arrived with 8,000 troops and was joined by reinforcements under Tachibana and Nabeshima,[3] while *Wani no jō rakujō no oboe* relates that:

> Ankokuji, a samurai lord from Chūgoku, with Kikkawa and Kobayakawa under his command, together with Chikushi Kōzuke of the Kyushu-shū, Nabeshima of Hizen, Tachibana Sakon and Sassa Mutsu-no-Kami, seven generals in all, arrived with men from thirteen provinces and took up positions for an attack.[4]

The names of the besieging generals are somewhat different on the map. They also call into question several other points of detail including the date

---

3 Kumamoto 2000, p. 64.
4 Kumamoto 2000, p. 431.

The Commander-in Chief of the besieging forces at Tanaka was Mōri Hidekane (1567–1601), the younger brother and adopted heir of Kobayakawa Takakage, who was only 20 years old. This hanging scroll of him is owned by the Gensaiji temple in Yamaguchi Prefecture. It is reproduced here by kind permission of the Chief Priest and was supplied by Yamaguchi City Board of Education Cultural Properties Protection Division.

of arrival, the identity of the Commander-in-Chief and his subordinates, the sources of their troops and the vital question of whether Sassa Narimasa was actually present at Tanaka.

Three cartouches at the bottom (western side) of the map contain abbreviated forms of the names of the Kishū-shū, the commanders associated with the Mōri family, who were originally from Kishū (Aki Province: modern Hiroshima Prefecture). Due west of the castle is the Commander-in Chief Mōri Hidekane to whom Hideyoshi gave charge of the besieging army at Tanaka at the tender age of 20. He was the ninth son of Mōri Motonari and the chosen heir of his older brother Kobayakawa Takakage, whom Hideyoshi had entrusted with the overall responsibility of crushing the Higo Rebellion. Takakage's adoption of Hidekane explains the use of the surname Kobayakawa for Hidekane in some accounts.[5] Hidekane had entered Hideyoshi's service following the peace settlement with the Mōri family. After service in the Kyushu campaign he became one of the generals whom Hideyoshi settled in its newly pacified provinces, receiving the 210,000 *koku* fief of Kurume in Chikugo Province. In later years Mōri Hidekane would stay faithful to Hideyoshi's heir, which led to the confiscation of his estates at the hands of the victorious Tokugawa after the 1600 Sekigahara campaign.

Next to Hidekane in a clockwise direction appears the name Miyoshi. This refers to Miyoshi Hirotaka (1538–1634), a retainer of the Mōri family who would also share in the defeat at Sekigahara in 1600, becoming a *rōnin* after the battle until finding service with the Asano family of Hiroshima. The other generals associated with the Mōri appear in one cartouche holding four names on the other side of the Hidekane cartouche in an anti-clockwise direction. The first is Hidekane's second in command at Tanaka: Ankokuji Ekei (1539–1600), an ordained Buddhist priest since childhood who had been chief negotiator on behalf of the Mōri when they reached their agreement with Hideyoshi in 1582. *Wani no jō rakujō no oboe* has him down erroneously as the Commander-in-Chief at Tanaka. Ekei went on to serve Hideyoshi and his heir with great loyalty until Sekigahara, where he was captured and later executed. The other names are three more retainers of the Mōri. Kuriya Shirōbei's dates of birth and death are unknown. Koshi may refer to a former retainer of the Amako family whom the Mōri defeated, but Hino cannot be identified any further.

The cartouches to the north of the castle are labelled Hizen-shū, and are the units drawn from the general area of Hizen Province, although the

---

5 Kunitake 1993, p. 120.

troops are not under the command of anyone from the Ryūzōji family. Their leader is instead Nabeshima Naoshige (1537–1619), who benefited greatly from the death of his former master Ryūzōji Takanobu at the hands of the Shimazu in 1584. Naoshige became independent and would eventually take over the Ryūzōji's own castle of Saga in 1590. Unlike the generals previously mentioned, he would finish on the winning side at Sekigahara. Also within the Hizen-shū are the names in the cartouche at the southerly tip of the castle lines that reads 'Oda Ise' and probably indicates family members of the later Oda Sōkō of Hizen province who had died in 1585. Three of them were killed at Tanaka, and 'Ise' probably denotes the honorary title of Ise-no-Kami.[6]

The next names on the plan are the Chikugo-shū of Chikugo Province. First is the formidable Tachibana Muneshige (1567–1642) of Yanagawa castle. Muneshige was the son of Takahashi Jōun, who had perished at the hands of the Shimazu when they captured his castle of Iwaya in 1586. As the adopted heir of the Tachibana he had already been very active in attempting to suppress the Higo Rebellion, and it was his supply column that had been attacked by the rebels as it left Jōmura. He too would be on the losing side during the Sekigahara campaign in 1600 but was reinstated in his domains not long afterwards when Ieyasu consolidated the balance of power in Kyushu. Due east of the castle is a cartouche bearing the name of Chikushi. This identifies Chikushi Hirokado (1556–1623), who submitted to Hideyoshi during the invasion of Kyushu and was allowed to retain his lands in Chikugo. He continued to serve the Toyotomi family and became a *rōnin* for a short time after Sekigahara.[7] In the eastern quarter are the Chikuzen-shū under the name Takahashi, which refers to Takahashi Mototane (1571–1614), the second son of Akizuki Tanezane of Chikuzen Province. Mototane had been adopted by the late Takahashi Jōun. After the invasion of Kyushu the family were rewarded by Hideyoshi with the 20,000 *koku* fief of Nobeoka in Hyūga Province. He too would be on the losing side at Sekigahara and would suffer banishment as a result.

The besieging commanders at Tanaka were therefore all staunch Hideyoshi loyalists who had either submitted to him prior to 1587 or joined him during the Kyushu invasion. All received recognition for their services in Kyushu ranging from having landholdings confirmed or being rapidly transferred to Kyushu with greatly increased wealth and responsibility as Hideyoshi's 'potted plants'. All but Nabeshima Naoshige would stay loyal to Hideyoshi as the years went by, and all would suffer in some way at Sekigahara. Where the information on the map differs from the lists in the chronicles lies first in the statement that these besiegers were drawn from 'thirteen provinces' as the *Wani no jō rakujō no oboe* relates, but the greatest revelation is one very important point that contradicts both chronicles. The map shows quite clearly that Sassa Narimasa, whose disobedience to Hideyoshi had brought on the Higo Rebellion, was not there in person, but this is perfectly understandable. While the Tanaka siege was in operation several other rebel actions were continuing, most notably at Jōmura, and Sassa's headquarters of Kumamoto

---

6 Mikawa 1999, p. 18.
7 Mikawa 1999, pp. 17–19.

could not be left undefended, so the disgraced Narimasa is more than likely to have been at one of those places early in the siege.[8] When Tanaka fell he was definitely in Yatsushiro Castle, as is confirmed by a letter sent there that was written to him reporting the army's success.[9]

The Besieging Units' Locations

Much of the written material on the left side of the map concerns the besieging army's dispositions.[10] The first piece of information is the overall space they occupied, which is stated to be an area of which the circumference was 50 *chō*, or 5.45 km. Had that perimeter been a perfect circle that would give an area with a radius of about eight *chō* (867 metres) as measured from the centre of the *honmaru*. This is more than sufficient as an estimate, although none of the units was actually stationed further away than five *chō* from the central point. *Wani Gundan* states that the 'insignificant little castle' was confined within an outer perimeter of five *chō*. This cannot mean a circumference because it is one-tenth of the circumference given on the map. However, if it is read as 'within a perimeter lying at a distance of five *chō* from the castle' it tallies well with the map.[11] There are however certain minor discrepancies. For example, the resulting plan shows that Nabeshima Naoshige was furthest away from the castle at five *chō* (545m). This may be taken as the rearmost point of Naoshige's unit within a narrow frontage because the named place is only four *chō* away. The only other major question concerns the Tachibana unit, who are stated on the map as being stationed five *chō* away. They appear instead to have been situated at a place that is two *chō* away, the only unit to be so close to the castle.[12] Tachibana Muneshige's location is further described in *Wani no jō rakujō no oboe* as being opposite the Hiakeguchi entrance to the castle.

As to the units' precise locations, the names of the places are not included on the map, only the distances from the castle, so we have to turn back to the chronicles. *Wani Gundan* simply provides a list of place names.[13] *Wani no jō rakujō no oboe* links a similar list of places to the names of the commanders, although there are major differences from the map concerning where they were based.[14] Two attempts have been made in the past whereby the units have been placed on to a modern map using the distances from the castle indicated on the battle plan, but unfortunately the two resulting diagrams differ greatly from one another. One is included in the 1999 report on the archaeological excavation where the approximate positions are suggested over a broad area.[15] The other is by Kunitake, who places the contingents

---

8   Mikawa 1999, p. 33.
9   Araki 2012, p. 104.
10   Mikawa 1997, p. 203.
11   Kumamoto 2000, p. 64.
12   Kunitake 1993, p. 147; Mikawa 1997, p. 24.
13   Kumamoto 2000, p. 64.
14   Kumamoto 2000, p. 431.
15   Mikawa 1999, p. 61.

very precisely on a modern map and includes photographs of the presumed locations.[16]

My own interpretation is shown below, where I have superimposed the probable locations for the besieging units on to a modern 1/25,000 scale map of the area. It follows the information given on the map and is based on the assumption that the besiegers would choose to occupy the best high ground near to the named places to allow a good view of the castle and to assist in their own defence should they suffer a counter-attack. Archaeological investigations at some of these sites have provided evidence of the deliberate clearing of ground to create defensible terraces. As the siege of Tanaka lasted for some time the besieging camps are likely to have been quite extensive, with fences, towers and guarded entrances, much like the *tsukejiro* of Jōmura. Because of the dense woodland around Tanaka (much of which was planted only in modern times), few of the besieging locations now provide an uninterrupted view of the castle, and when seen from Tanaka itself the places appear only as forested hills. In almost every case, however, the strategic decision to occupy that particular point on the map is abundantly clear.

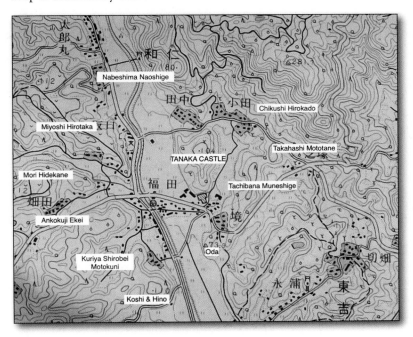

In this illustration the author has superimposed the probable locations of the attacking units on to a modern map of the Tanaka area. The five units that make up the Mōri family contribution are shown covering the castle to the west, of whom Mōri Hidekane and Ankokuji Ekei straddle the vital Nankan road to the west. Nabeshima Naoshige holds the north. The Chikuzen and Chikugo contingents face the castle from the east, while Oda, Koshi and Hino guard the approach from Kumamoto to the south.

The commander Mōri Hidekane was stationed to the west of the castle on the hills across the Wani River. His headquarters lay on the prominent hill at 112 metres above sea level just to the north of a settlement now called Hatakeda, from where he would have enjoyed the view of Tanaka Castle precisely as it appears on the drawing. Between Hidekane and the castle lay rice fields and the wide river bed. I have placed Hidekane's Second-in-

---

16 Kunitake, pp. 164–165.

Command Ankokuji Ekei on a hill immediately to the south of this with Kuriya Shirōbei on the next hill along, together with Miyoshi Hirotaka across another stream and a minor road to the north and Koshi and Hino further to the south. Whatever their precise locations may have been, these units that made up the Kishū-shū would have covered the vital Nankan Road that led to Ōtsuyama Iekado's hilltop fortress of Tsuzuragadake Castle 4.5 km away to the west on the summit of Ōtsuyama (256 metres), from where a fire beacon provided direct communication between Iekado and the barons of Tanaka.[17] This road would have been the most likely conduit for any relieving army and needed to be guarded.

In this view we are looking to the west from the ni-no-maru across the Shinshiro. In the distance is the road to Nankan and Ōtsuyama Iekado's Tsuzuragadake Castle, a likely route for any relieving army. It was covered from the round hill to its immediate left by the contingent under Ankokuji Ekei. Mōri Hidekane was stationed across the road to the north.

The northern side of the siege lines shows a similar concern for covering the roads that led away from Tanaka as well as choosing places from which to threaten the castle itself. Nabeshima Naoshige's widespread army dispositions guarded the road to the north along the Wani River past the Kumano Shrine, which is shown on the map using the conventional symbol for a *torii* gateway next to the name Wani 和仁. This road led eventually into Chikugo Province. Other troops from the Hizen-shū would have been situated on the lower slopes of Miyatake, the summit of which is indicated by the triangulation point of 281.7 metres. This was the tall forested mountain directly opposite Tanaka, from where they could look across at the hill's smaller namesake within the castle. Use would surely have been made of the lower peak at a spot height of 80 metres.

---

17 See the newsletter *Sengoku da yori* No. 8 (2008) p. 4 for the account of an experiment whereby a beacon was lit on Ōtsuyama and was seen in daylight by visitors to the Tanaka site.

Further round to the east, Chikushi Hirokado's troops were stationed on the slope of an unnamed hill that gave one of the best views of Tanaka. The garrison had recognised the importance of the location and had attempted in vain to prevent Hirokado from occupying it.[18] The Takahashi army lay not far away to the south, and together with Tachibana Muneshige covered the main Yamaga Road to the east which led towards the besieged castle of Jōmura 12 km away. Muneshige's position was the closest of all to Tanaka Castle and faced the Hiakeguchi across the Odagawa from the hill of Shibatsuka 柴塚. Finally, the Oda unit straddled the road to the south at Sakai 境, probably occupying the prominent hill that has a triangulation point of 73 metres. This southern approach, supported by Koshi and Hino across the river, followed the Wanigawa downstream in the general direction of Kumamoto Castle. All four points of the compass were therefore covered.

The northern side of Tanaka Castle is shown here looking from the section of the siege lines occupied by Nabeshima Naoshige's contingent. They were stationed on the hill of Miyadake seen on the immediate left behind the torii gateway of the Kumano Shrine, covering the road to the north and also the Wani River. Its course would have been much more extensive in 1587 and flowed then below the castle hill.

---

18   From a personal conversation with Kuroda Yūji, 22 April 2016.

A close-up of the V-shaped ditch that divides the western demaru from the ni-no-maru. Part of the ditch has been left in its unexcavated state. In the distance is the southern road towards Kumamoto and the positions occupied by Koshi and Hino.

The Besieging Army's Regulations

As well as having stout defences for their camps the besiegers also needed discipline, and the other main piece of information included on the left side of the map is entitled *Gunchū Hatto* (internal army ordinances); a summary of the overall regulations for the besieging forces. Its four short clauses are brief and to the point and show a considerable understanding of the mentality of the Japanese warrior, because in essence they are orders banning certain practices that would be deleterious to the overall success of the operation. They begin with Clause One: 'Item, concerning the matter of the prohibition of disputes', which is more simply translated as 'quarrels are forbidden'. This refers no doubt to matters of samurai pride that cause arguments, ranging from the right to be the first into the attack to squabbles over claims to severed heads. The second clause uses the archaic word *oka* (forceful buying), to ban the use of strong-arm tactics when trading with local people. There must be no bullying or intimidation to get a low price for foodstuffs and goods, because when the siege is over the local merchants and farmers must be left with a good impression of the noble army who have overcome the wicked rebels.

Clause Three deals with the vital matter of strategy and tactics and the need to avoid the pursuit of personal honour as: 'Item, tactics must be left to the decision of Ankokuji and Hidekane'. Independence of movement and manoeuvre are therefore not allowed, and no one's individual glory must take precedence over the army's common objectives, the achievement of which is the responsibility of the two commanders and no one else. They are the generals delegated by Hideyoshi to carry out all military operations against Tanaka and will also act as his *ikusa metsuke* (army superintendents): a role that oversees all matters of internal discipline. Finally, Clause Four adds: 'In addition: in matters of construction the above applies'. This extends the prohibition on individual manoeuvring to the erection of temporary buildings in the siege lines on a personal whim. In all things including this the orders of the commander-in-chief and his deputy are to be followed without any deviation.[19]

---

19 Reproduced in modern Japanese in Mikawa 1997, p. 203 and further discussed in Mikawa 1999, pp. 25–26.

8

The Battle of Tanaka

With Hideyoshi's generals arranged outside the castle and the defenders crammed inside it the battle of Tanaka was about to begin. *Wani Gundan* suggests that Mōri Hidekane expected it to be a short operation, because it states that Hidekane was so confident that Tanaka would fall at the first assault that he had prepared no siege equipment.[1] This expectation was to prove incorrect, so the Tanaka operation may be usefully divided into three stages: the initial assault; the month-long siege and the final successful attack.

The First Attack on Tanaka

Hidekane's army had arrived outside Tanaka on 10m 16d (25 November). They spent two weeks setting up the lines described above, after which the initial assault took place at the Hour of the Dragon (07:00) on 11m 2d (1 December 1587), and both war tales relate that hostilities only began once a spirited display of single combat had concluded.[2] This was an anachronistic way of commencing a battle that was based on the cherished myth that in the days of their ancestors all the fighting had been conducted between honourable opponents who had sought out suitable victims by issuing a verbal challenge that included a proclamation of their pedigrees. Legend had it that such a challenge would have only been accepted by someone worthy, who would then ride out and give battle. The two samurai would then fight to the death with no one being allowed to disturb their deadly and honourable duty. Notwithstanding the fact that the conditions during even small medieval encounters must have made such situations highly unlikely at any time, by 1587 the presence of large armies that included organised weapon groups made such behaviour virtually impossible in the heat of battle. It was, however, still practicable if performed before battle was joined, and could be a considerable morale-booster for the winning side. It is therefore easy to accept the statement that the battle of Tanaka began with just such an

---

1   Kumamoto 2000, p. 64.
2   Oyama 2003, p. 106.

encounter as an heroic curtain-raiser for the serious business of a mass attack on the castle.

According to *Wani Gundan* the opening single combat at Tanaka was initiated by one of the besiegers: a samurai called Matsubara Gorōemon Naomoto, who rode up to the edge of the castle's ditch and issued a challenge in suitably heroic terms. It was answered and accepted by Haruno Tōya, one of the Wani's senior retainers, who gave an appropriately scornful reply and galloped out to meet him. Unlike the mounted combats of the twelfth-century Gempei War where bows and arrows were the primary weapons of choice, Gorōemon and Tōya fought from horseback with spears. There must have been several violent clashes, because the fight only ended when both their spear shafts bent and snapped in the middle at the same time, depositing both men on the ground. Winded and exhausted the champions disengaged and sat on the ground 'like two dogs tired out after a fight'.[3]

After this heroic encounter the first serious attack began, but details of it are sadly lacking. It appears that Hideyoshi's army experienced intense fire from the castle as they moved up within range, and according to *Wani Gundan* the Tanaka defenders then sallied out of the castle to engage them. The accounts suggest that the besiegers came off worse with one hundred casualties compared to only four sustained by the defence who had 'one or two wounds', and not one was killed.[4] Local tradition relates that so many of the attackers were slaughtered along Tachibana Muneshige's south-eastern sector that the little Odagawa ran red with blood and would later be called the Chinamigawa (bloody wave river) by local people.[5] It is easy to envisage the scene whereby the Tachibana, Chikushi and Takahashi contingents poured down from their forested hills across the flat rice fields to face a hail of bullets and arrows from Tanaka's rocky eastern face.

Hidekane's army then pulled back to their prepared positions. The first day's engagement had demonstrated very clearly that Tanaka could not be overcome by a quick assault, so a major reconsideration took place among the besieging commanders. Their previous haughty rejection of siege equipment was soon reversed and the second phase of the campaign began, although it is impossible to ascertain at which precise stage of the operation this decision was made. There may have been many more attacks and many more casualties among the besiegers; the records are silent on this point. The fact was that a small *okajiro* was driving off every assault made upon it, and the resulting change of strategy represented a huge compliment to the tenacity of the Wani family and their supporters.

Mōri Hidekane's second plan of attack was designed to seal the castle off completely from the outside world, allowing no defender to escape and no relieving force to enter. It was a strategy used by Hideyoshi himself on several occasions such as at the huge *yamashiro* of Tottori in 1581, where the defenders may even have resulted to cannibalism after a prolonged 200 day siege. A similar blockade was of course already under way at Jōmura and had

3   Kumamoto 2000, p. 64.
4   Kunitake 1993, p. 117.
5   Kunitake 1993, pp. 143–144.

On the left of this picture is the lower eastern section of Tanaka Castle known as the Hiake Yashiki. The crash barrier indicates the present location of the Oda River. The hills around held the Chikugo and Chikuzen contingents, and it is easy to imagine them pouring across the flat fields to launch the first attack on Tanaka.

reached a stalemate, but the small size of Tanaka compared to Jōmura may have encouraged the besiegers to think that a solution could be achieved at Tanaka with minimal losses to the besiegers, so the twofold perimeter fence shown so clearly on the map was now built to enclose the castle in a tight and effective palisade.

The two Wani chronicles make no reference to the construction of the perimeter fence. It is however mentioned in one of Hideyoshi's letters, and the discovery of the battle map has confirmed its existence beyond all doubt, because the enclosing palisade is prominently drawn on the picture and is shown crossing the Wanigawa at two places. There are 12 simple gateways to allow the entry of attacking parties, although there appears to be no deliberate passageway through the inner line of the fence, which is shown in weaker outline. Hideyoshi refers to its role and the change of strategy in a letter to Ankokuji Ekei and Kobayakawa Takakage dated 12m 10d (8 January 1588). He fully appreciates the effect on the rest of the population of Kyushu if the rebels at Tanaka are not crushed, and notes starkly that the purpose of the palisade is literally 'to starve the animals to death' (*hoshigoroshi*).

The Higo rebels Wani and Hebaru are surrounded and it is a time of freezing weather, but even though they may be suffering from illness, is an attack, even by someone of Takakage's reputation really the thing that will crush them? Accordingly we have built a stout double *mogari* fence to starve the animals to death. Not one must escape, or it will be noticed throughout Kyushu in the time to come.[6]

---

6   Mikawa 1997, pp. 316–317; Oyama 2003, pp. 102–103.

In this letter the double fence is described as being of the *mogari* (cloud of wild geese)style. According to military historian Sasama Yoshihiko, a *mogari* was a defensive line made from sharpened bamboo. In separate books he provides illustrations of two varieties: one protruding from the ground at about waist height, and a more elaborate version where sharpened bamboo is packed densely into a ditch.[7] The former is more likely for a hurriedly constructed siege line. We may therefore envisage the Tanaka double fence as a sturdy gated palisade outside a weaker bamboo *mogari* that acted like a primitive version of barbed wire in that it would hinder and delay, rather than totally prevent an assailant's passage. The attacking army, of course, could easily remove sections of it in front of the gates for their assaults, while any defenders trying to so the same would come under fire from the outer fence.

The Last Days of Tanaka

Tanaka Castle was now sealed off from the outside world, but instead of describing the decision to erect the palisade or any actions around it, *Wani Gundan* simply ignores a month of siege warfare and lets the narrative jump ahead to the third and final phase of the campaign. The events of the intervening month are therefore lost to history apart from the brief reference to the fence in Hideyoshi's letter and the mention in the same missive of the garrison withstanding extremes of cold and illness.[8] From other sieges of the time we may suppose that raids were carried out by both sides and that any attempts at relief were intercepted. What is clear from subsequent events, however, is that whatever privations the garrison may have suffered during December 1587 they were no nearer to surrender. In spite of all Mōri Hidekane's efforts the castle was still holding out a month after the initial assault. It had its own well for water and was still sufficient in food and ammunition. Morale was high and the besiegers were getting desperate, so Hidekane's plans changed yet again.

The fine details of the third and final phase of the siege may now be inferred following the discovery of the battle map, which I believe was drawn at this stage in the campaign, not at the time of the army's arrival. The latter option is almost completely ruled out anyway by the depiction of the palisade, yet rather than being just a static depiction of the siege lines at any given time during the eleventh lunar month of 1587, two pieces of relevant information on the map suggest that it is in fact a snapshot of the moment of decision by Mōri Hidekane to launch the final assault on the castle.

The first pieces of information to support this theory are the remaining items of written material on the left side of the map, which read: 'Item: four attack routes (*shiyori yon guchi*); the Kishū-shū *hitokuchi*, the Hizen-shū *hitokuchi*, the Tachibana *hitokuchi* and the Chikushi *hitokuchi*. In other

7   Sasama, Yoshihiko, *Buke senjin sahō shūsei* (Tokyo: Yūzankaku, 1968), p. 320; Sasama, Yoshihiko, *Zusetsu Nihon kassen bugu jiten* (Tokyo: Kashiwashobō, 2004), p. 189.
8   Oyama 2003, pp. 102–103.

words, one 'approach' (*hitokuchi*) is identified for each of the four major units present in the lines. The map is therefore an actual plan of attack, not just a useful map of the siege lines. The other piece of relevant information is added to the drawing of the castle, and consists of the word *shiyoru*仕寄る (attack) written in two places that correspond to the targets for the Nabeshima and Tachibana sectors. These inscriptions may have been intended to give greater precision to the advances by these units, implying that the other attacks from the east and west would be more general advances against their nearest sectors.

The first of the two specified places is the *demaru* of Miyatake that covered the North Gate. Nabeshima Naoshige, I believe, is being ordered to secure this important way into the castle rather than dissipating his efforts against the cliff of Iwa Jizō or the steep terraces on the northern side. The second is even more interesting, because the word 'attack' is written above the drawing of the detached s*an no maru*, the long and narrow southern *demaru*. It was noted earlier that on the map the fence built by the defenders passes inside this vulnerable 'ravelin', which includes an openwork wooden tower similar to those shown for the *honmaru*, as was confirmed by the archaeological study.[9] Kuroda's theory is that the southern *demaru* was either captured or abandoned early in the siege and that the tower was built not by the defenders but by the besiegers to give them an elevated firing position into the *ni no maru*.[10] The men constructing it would have had to be protected by wooden shields and may well have worked under the cover of darkness, with any casualties being compensated for by the advantage given to the army by the possession of the *demaru*. A walk across the excavated site shows just how close the two sides were at this point, which would have been the shortest gap of no man's land during the whole of the siege of Tanaka. If Kuroda's theory is true the word '*shiyoru*' means that the crucial assault is to be launched not against the southern *demaru*, but from it.

The precise nature of the four attack routes also suggests a desire to rush large numbers of troops into the castle in a coordinated fashion when a signal was given rather than a slower all-round assault from many different places. *Wani Gundan* confirms that just such a signal was expected, because the new scheme envisaged the all-out attack on the castle taking place after it had been mortally wounded from within by treachery. The moment to advance would be revealed by the sight of a fire beacon lit by the man whom the besiegers regarded as the weak point in the castle's command: Hebaru Noto-no-Kami Chikayuki, the husband of the Wani brothers' elder sister and the man entrusted with the defence of the inner sanctum of the *honmaru*. The army numbers show that Chikayuki had command of one-third of the castle garrison, and their defection, perhaps accompanied by an act of sabotage, might well have been enough to allow the successful entry of the besieging army.

The first communication between Mōri Hidekane and Hebaru Chikayuki suggesting the treacherous plot was made by means of an arrow letter loosed into the castle, and the offer Hidekane made was the restoration of half of

---

9   Kuroda 2005, pp. 5–6.
10   From a personal conversation with Kuroda Yūji on 22 April 2016.

Chikayuki's former landholdings.[11] That does not seem like much of a reward for a serious act of treason, but in Sengoku Japan alliances – even between brothers-in-law – could be built on sand, and the example of Ōtsuyama Sukefuyu noted in an earlier chapter shows how readily the barons of Higo changed allegiance when it suited them. Hebaru Chikayuki may well have believed that the castle was certain to fall, at which point he would lose his head in the cause of his wife's family, so was it not a wiser course of action to abandon the Wani to their fate? Perhaps Chikayuki even sensed that the times were changing; that the *jizamurai* exemplified by the defiant Wani brothers had had their day and that the future belonged to the virtually professional soldiers who now besieged him and to whose status he may well have aspired. If he betrayed the family he would be reconfirmed in his fief as Sassa Narimasa's *yoriki,* and the Hebaru would prosper as Sassa retainers rather than being obliterated.

The besiegers' plot, however, went far beyond mere defection. What was being asked of Hebaru Chikayuki surpassed sabotage and was the most drastic act of treason that was possible: the assassination of his brother-in-law Wani Chikazane. Both chronicles take pains to point out that the actual murder was committed by someone else, but Hebaru Chikayuki agreed to this act of enormity as part of the scheme. According to *Wani Gundan* Chikayuki promised that when the deed was done he would give a signal to that effect

The southern demaru or san-no-maru (third bailey) is one of the most interesting features of the Tanaka site, partly because the defensive fence runs between it and the inner baileys. It was probably connected to the ni-no-maru by means of a narrow bridge. During the siege it held a wooden tower, which may have been built under fire by the besiegers.

---

11 Kunitake 1993, pp. 123–125.

by means of a fire beacon, and these intentions were somehow conveyed to Mōri Hidekane. The *Wani Gundan* account implies a rapidly moving series of events from that moment onwards, although it is more than likely that the plans took some time to develop and involved further secret negotiations, because *Wani no jō rakujō no oboe* mentions smuggling Chikayuki's seven-year-old son out of the castle to be presented to Ankokuji Ekei as a hostage. This may have been insisted upon by the besiegers as a pledge of compliance, but by providing a hostage Chikayuki was also guaranteeing the survival of the Hebaru family if everything else went wrong.

From this point onwards the siege of Tanaka castle moved rapidly to its close. Hebaru Chikayuki found his assassin in the person of a retainer of the Wani called Usono Kurōdo, who is said to have borne a grudge against Chikazane because he had been passed over for promotion. In the middle of the night or at early dawn (the accounts differ) Kurōdo, whose presence near his lord would have attracted little suspicion, sneaked into Chikazane's sleeping quarters and stabbed him to death. As soon as the deed was confirmed Hebaru Chikayuki informed his followers of their change of allegiance, lit the fire beacon and pulled his men out of the *honmaru*, which was then set on fire. This final and very drastic element in the plot may have been a decision taken on the spur of the moment rather than being part of the original plan, because a high wind ensured that the whole area of the two inner baileys was soon engulfed in flames. The Wani were therefore forced to evacuate the inner baileys and meet the attack from the detached sections, as is clearly suggested by the accounts in the chronicles because all the subsequent fighting is described as taking place around the western *demaru,* the North Gate and the Shinshiro.

The pivotal event of the annual battle re-enactment at Tanaka is the death of Wani Chikazane, although in the drama the murderer performing the deed is identified as Hebaru Chikayuki. Note the crane motif which is supposed to have been the mon (family badge) of the Wani family.

The Final Assault

Upon realising that his elder brother had been murdered Wani Danjō Chikanori assumed command of Tanaka Castle and tried to rally the survivors, but a rapid assessment of the situation showed him that all was lost, so the next decision he took was to ensure the safety of the women and children from the Wani family. It turned out, however, that his younger brother Jinki had already anticipated such a course of action and had taken charge of the murdered Chikazane's pregnant wife and five-year-old daughter and placed them into the care of the family's senior retainer Haruno Tōya. Somehow Tōya managed to get them out of the castle while the attack was in progress and conveyed them to the nearby Wani family temple of Tōshōji. He then instructed a priest called Seichō to escort them as quickly as possible over the mountains to Miike, where they would be safe with the Ono family. When Seichō set off with them Haruno Tōya plunged back into the midst of the enemy and was killed. His efforts would prove successful, because the women made it safely to Miike and Wani Chikazane's son was born six months later. He was adopted by his uncle Ono Munezane and given the name Ono Sakuzaemon Shigezane, so through him the Wani bloodline continued.

Danjō's own wife, a 13-year-old girl known to posterity as Wani Gozen, was not so fortunate, and her sad fate is included in *Wani Gundan,* although there are certain variations on the story.[12] She fled the castle much later than the other women, possibly because she had taken an active personal role in the fighting. *Wani Gundan* relates that Chikazane's wife had already left for Miike before Wani Gozen and other female companions managed to reach the Tōshōji, and that the now abandoned temple had been set on fire by the besiegers. With no other sanctuary available to them the desperate women decided to commit suicide by throwing themselves into the Wani River with their children in their arms. Wani Gozen made three attempts to drown herself but was washed ashore every time. Eventually the current caught her body and carried her three *ri* (12 km) downstream to the confluence of the Wani River with the wider Kikuchi River near the village of Uchida. Her body sank beneath the waves for the last time, and her lifeless corpse was eventually washed up beside a rock that would later be called the Wani Ishi. The local people enshrined her as the deity Wani Gozen in the shrine called the Wani Ishigū that still stands on the hill overlooking the river.

Because of the nature of her tragic death she became a *kami* of water, and at times of drought prayers would be offered to her spirit. Local tradition states that every year during the summer months the farmers hear a faintly booming drum that indicates the return of Wani Gozen and the bringing of rain. A different account of the women's suicides includes the wife of Hebaru Hōki-no-kami, said to be the younger brother of the traitor Chikayuki. This may of course have been a mistaken reference to Chikayuki's own wife, who

---

12 They are presented in a published report about the archaeological investigation of Wani Ishizan castle where her shrine still stands. Nagomi Town, *Wani Ishisan shiro ato* (Nagomi: Nagomi Board of Education, 2007), pp. 3–5.

The Kikuchi River at Uchida, showing the approximate location where the body of Wani Gozen was washed ashore. She was the wife of Wani Danjō Chikanori and tried to drown herself when Tanaka Castle fell.

The Wani Ishigū stands high above the Kikuchi River and enshrines Wani Gozen as the local kami (deity) of water. At times of drought prayers are offered to her spirit, and local tradition states that every year during the summer months the farmers hear a faintly booming drum that indicates the return of Wani Gozen and the bringing of rain.

would surely have been inclined to put an end to herself after what had happened.[13]

The Last of the Wani

By now all semblance of order had disappeared within the burning castle, so the senior members of the Wani household resolved to perish gloriously and leave their names to posterity. This intention was naturally matched by an equal determination on the part of numerous individual besiegers to be the one who would gain great glory by taking the noble head of a Wani brother or a senior family retainer. The first of the brothers to be mentioned in this context was the bear-like Jinki, who chose to suffer a heroic death and did not have long to wait for his opportunity. Hoping for the honour of taking Jinki's prestigious head, a high-ranking mounted samurai in Hideyoshi's army called Tsuda Yohei galloped up and confronted him. Jinki slashed back at his assailant with his sword and cut the man almost in two from the peak of his helmet to his groin. Undaunted, others tried their luck, and Jinki received a further challenge from Ushijima Fujishichi from the Hizen force.

It is at this point in the narrative that we encounter the second of the victims whose deaths would lead them to being enshrined as local guardian *kami*, because Ushijima Fujishichi was joined by Yufu Ōinosuke Korekiyo,

This plain enclosed two-storey gatehouse at Torigoe Castle is a likely model for the strongest gates at Tanaka because it provides cover for sharpshooters. It has a small postern gate on either side of the main entrance and is integrated with the solid wooden fence.

---

13   Kumamoto 2000, p. 66; Nagomi 2007, pp. 3–4.

a retainer of Tachibana Muneshige. This alone shows that the castle must have been overrun by this point, because two separate attacking armies are now totally mixed up. Yufu Ōinosuke rode forward to challenge Wani Jinki, but one of Nakamura Jibushōyū's archers, who was acting as a sharpshooter and was concealed from view, loosed an arrow at him. It pierced Ōinosuke's breastplate and went through as far as the middle of his back so that he fell dead from his horse. *Wani Gundan* makes no reference to the strong local tradition associated with Ōinosuke's death that appears in *Higo Kokushi* of 1706 and is recounted by both Araki and Oyama. It relates that when he rode up to challenge Jinki, Ōinosuke's followers suspected that he might be heading into a trap and called out to him to return, but Ōinosuke was deaf so did not hear them. As his retainers feared, the hidden marksman put an arrow into him. The incident also provides a clue towards visualising the structure of Tanaka's gates, because Jinki was stationed at the North Gate, and the enclosed upper storey of a gatehouse would be the most likely place for an archer to have operated effectively without being seen.

Yufu Ōinosuke is the only victim of the Tanaka siege to be enshrined on the battlefield itself. His grave lies to the south-east of the castle site at Shibatsuka among a grove of bamboo to the rear of the location of Tachibana Muneshige's headquarters. Because of his deafness and its influence on the manner of his death he is enshrined there as a *kami* of the ears.[14] Offerings for help with hearing problems are still made to his spirit in the form of piles of *hifukidake*, short tubes of bamboo that have a small hole through a node at one end; they are traditionally used for blowing life into a smouldering fire.[15]

Meanwhile, Ujishima Fujishichi continued his advance against Jinki in spite of the death of his comrade, but was tackled by the senior Wani retainer Matsuo Hyūga and fought a single combat. They appear to have lost all their weapons in the fight because they grappled furiously, which led to them both falling to their deaths off the cliff of Iwa Jizō. Hyūga's son Matsuo Ichinokami and fellow retainer Ishihara Gyōbu were also severely wounded at this time. With all his followers either scattered or dead, the bear-like Wani Jinki Chikamune faced down 20 assailants and in spite of a hand wound cut down the eight nearest to him and drove off seven others, then rode off into the mountains alone. 'It is not known,' says the author of *Wani Gundan*, 'whether he lived or died'.[16]

Other accounts provide a possible answer to the question of Jinki's fate. In these versions he is said not merely to have disappeared but to have escaped from the castle and then committed suicide next to the grave of his wife, whose sad story begins when Jinki was sent by his father in 1578 to pay homage to Ōtomo Sōrin. Jinki's striking appearance caught the eyes of the Bungo court, and when he left for Higo he took home gifts in the form of 31 muskets and a woman described as a *namban-jō* ('Southern Barbarian girl'). She is supposed

14 Oyama 2003, pp. 109–110; Araki 2012, p. 79.

15 Yufu's status as the local *kami* of hearing makes his gravesite one of eight shrines in the Nagomi area that specialise in the health of different bodily parts. They are unique for being found as a cluster and enshrine the *kami* of vitality, eyes, teeth, ears, warts, the stomach, limbs, and reproduction, although none of the others have any connection with the battle.

16 Kumamoto 2000, p. 65.

The grave of Yufu Ōinosuke Korekiyo lies to the south-east of Tanaka Castle. He was a retainer of the Tachibana and was killed by an arrow delivered by a concealed archer. Yufu was deaf, so he had not heard the warning shouted to him by his followers. He is now enshrined here as the kami of hearing, and offerings are made to his spirit for help with deafness.

to have been Portuguese or Spanish and was brought to Japan because of the Ōtomo's Christian connections, even though that is highly unlikely to have happened. The girl was warmly welcomed at Tanaka Castle where she was referred to in honourable terms as Namban-sama, but the comparatively rough living conditions did not suit her and after two years she fell ill with a cold and died. She was buried near to the Wani family temple and after the fall of the castle Wani Jinki committed suicide next to her grave. The story continues to say that they left behind a daughter known as Namban-ge ('Southern Barbarian Hair').[17] Any personal colouration was however probably derived from Jinki's own unusual complexion rather than European ancestry.

After Jinki had disappeared Wani Danjō Chikanori was the last of the three brothers left standing at Tanaka. Another giant of a man, he carried an extra-long *nodachi* sword with a 1.45 metre-long blade. With it, says *Wani Gundan*, he cut down the enemies surrounding him 'as if harvesting rice, flax, bamboo or reeds'. More and more soldiers approached, but this proved to be to his advantage because the assailants began to trample each other underfoot as they tried to close with him. Danjō turned away from them and ascended the hill of Miyatake within the castle. Jimbō Gorō and Sugino Mataichi from Hideyoshi's army mistakenly thought he was fleeing and set off

---

17 Oyama 2003, pp. 128–132.

The statue of Wani Danjō Chikanori at Tanaka Castle. Instead of the sword shown in the statue, he is said to have used a *nodachi* (extra-long sword) that is described being used during his last moments in *Wani Gundan*.

after him. Danjō saw them coming, at which he took his *nodachi* and threw it away. He then spread his arms widely and as the two samurai reached him he seized them. With the two men held under his armpits, Danjō dived off the edge of Miyatake into the valley below, and all three were killed.[18]

18 Kumamoto 2000, p. 65.

The written sources for the battle are in conflict over the fate of the five senior retainers of the Wani. In *Wani Gundan* only the two brothers are mentioned as being killed with no reference to any deaths among their immediate followers other than the self-sacrifice of Haruno Tōya after he had taken the women to safety. In *Wani no jō rakujō no oboe* however, Matsuo Hyūga and his son Matsuo Ichinokami perform several meritorious deeds, until finally they too are struck down and die. However, Kusano Hayato (the captain of the *ukimusha*) and Nakamura Jibushōyū are not mentioned anywhere as being killed, and the chief retainer Ishihara Gyōbu may also have escaped, even though *Higo Kokushi* of 1706 adds his name to the list of the dead.[19]

Oyama believes that Ishihara Gyōbu survived because other accounts describe him in his later years as being furious at having failed to kill the traitor Hebaru Chikayuki. On this reasoning Ishihara must have survived the battle and tried to hunt Chikayuki down but never caught up with him.[20] A fuller version of Ishihara Gyōbu's fate comes from a descendant of his in the eleventh generation who told Oyama that it was his ancestor, not Haruno Tōya or any priest of the Tōshōji, who took charge of Wani Chikazane's wife when the castle fell. They escaped from the burning fortress together, but instead of heading straight for Miike they hid in a cave for five months to avoid the search for survivors that was being carried out. The cave was never discovered, and every day in their fastness they would face in the direction of Tanaka Castle, put their hands together and recite the *nembutsu* prayer. The pair eventually made it to Miike and the safety of the Ono family, and Oyama's informant told him that as late as the Meiji Period some descendants of the Wani who had settled in Yanagawa with the Ono family would journey to the site of Tanaka Castle to remember their ancestors.[21] When he eventually died the brave Ishihara Gyōbu was buried in the Wani Valley, along with the other two known survivors of the battle from the ranks of the senior retainers: Kusano Hayato and Nakamura Jibushōyū. Their graves can still be identified and are cared for to this day.[22]

The Fall of Tanaka Castle

The precise date of the fall of Tanaka Castle differs between the two chronicles. In *Wani Gundan* the assassin Usuno Kurōdo enters Chikazane's sleeping quarters at midnight on 12m 6d (4 January 1588), so on that basis the fall of the castle is regarded as having taken place during the following day: 12m 7d (5 January 1588).[23] *Wani no jō rakujō no oboe* however has Chikayuki sending his son out as a hostage at early dawn of the previous 12m 5d (3 January) and sets the death of Chikazane at the Hour of the Snake (09:00)

---

19 Oyama 2003, p. 127.
20 Oyama 2003, p. 135.
21 Oyama 2003, pp. 136–137.
22 Oyama 2003, pp. 127–128.
23 Kumamoto 2000, p. 64.

that same morning. In this version the battle must have been completed by nightfall because it states that by dawn of 12m 6d Hebaru Chikayuki has left the general area of the castle and is heading for Hizen province.[24]

Two letters sent immediately after the battle support the *Wani no jō rakujō no oboe* date. The first is from Sassa Masamoto, a near relative of Sassa Narimasa, and is addressed to two retainers of the Sagara. It refers to the castle falling 'yesterday, the fifth day'. The same letter also provides chilling confirmation that a massacre took place, because, 'There are no survivors among either men or women. There has a been a clean sweep, a wholesale slaughter' (*nadegiri*).[25] The second letter is a report sent by Ankokuji Ekei to Sassa Narimasa, who was currently residing in Yatsushiro. It is dated 12m 7d and referring to the fall of the castle 'on the day before yesterday'.[26] It would therefore appear most likely that the sequence of events began before dawn on 12m 5d (3 January) and were effectively over by the end of the same day, although the story of Ishihara Gyōbu hiding in a cave suggests that a 'mopping-up operation' continued for some time afterwards.

The same letter to Sassa Narimasa also confirms Hebaru Chikayuki's treachery by stating that as a result of his loyalty to Narimasa he was to be given back half his original landholdings, but *Wani Gundan* states that the promised restoration of half of Chikayuki's fief was never honoured, so that he was forced to wander the countryside and eventually returned to the Wani area where he eventually died of illness. He is definitely buried there, because his grave occupies a far from obscure position in sight of the road leading towards Tanaka Castle. His rehabilitation complete, fresh flowers are still placed on his grave to this day. It may seem surprising that the man whose treachery brought about the destruction of the Wani family is buried so close to the castle and is so honoured, but in his change of heart Hebaru Chikayuki had behaved no differently from any other floating warrior.

Chikayuki's enshrinement in the Tanaka area may also reflect a desire to keep his spirit placated lest he become that most terrible of things: an angry ghost. A persistent Japanese belief states that when a person dies a violent or untimely death he remains possessed by the worldly passion in which he died. Vengeful spirits such as dead samurai slaughtered on battlefields provide rich material for the numerous ghost stories and plays that make up many Noh and Kabuki dramas. Because of his enshrinement the traitor Hebaru Chikayuki therefore met a peaceful end, but a different fate was in store for Usono Kurōdo. He was despised by all because of the assassination and was forced to become a beggar, eventually dying of starvation at the roadside.[27] If a shrine was ever raised to placate him its location is unrecorded.

So ended the great siege of Tanaka Castle. The former Wani domain was given temporarily to Tachibana Muneshige pending a final settlement of the Higo Rebellion. He kept a watchful eye on the area from Yanagawa Castle and regularly intervened against the surviving rebels over the coming months.

---

24 Kumamoto 2000, p. 431.
25 Mikawa 1997, pp. 206–207 & 314–315.
26 Kunitake 1993, pp. 124–125; Mikawa 1997 pp. 208–209 & 315.
27 Kumamoto 2000, p. 66.

Meanwhile Toyotomi Hideyoshi was informed about the fall of Tanaka by means of a letter from Kobayakawa Takakage on 12m 6d (4 January 1588).[28] Hideyoshi wrote back with congratulations twice in separate letters dated 12m 27d (25 January), and in both of them he gives hints of his future plans for the resettlement of Higo. The first letter is the longer and makes reference separately to all the rebel groups. The relevant parts with regard to Tanaka are as follows:

> Item, in the matter of Wani and Hebaru, in fulfilment of my orders to cut off their heads, not one has escaped. Accordingly, among those killed the heads of four of their number have been presented. Indeed, I think you have served to the very best of your ability. In particular, Kobayakawa Takakage's loyalty is most gratifying. Continue to serve with loyalty from now on…
>
> Item, furthermore, search out and locate the families of the people who participated in the current uprising, then punish them with my blessing. It doesn't matter if the province is devastated. Punish those who were swayed to take part in the uprising, those who did not serve with loyalty in the present war, those who did not set out to war and those who sat on the fence. Next spring, discuss it with the *jōshi* (envoys).
>
> I thank you for the hardships you have endured through being encamped in the middle of winter, may your loyalty never be exhausted.[29]

It is perhaps surprising to see that fresh flowers are still offered at the grave of Hebaru Chikayuki, who betrayed Tanaka Castle. He was responsible for the death of Wani Chikazane and the destruction of Tanaka, yet in doing so his behaviour was no more than an extreme version of the normal attitudes embraced by the 'floating warriors'.

28 Oyama 2003, p. 139.
29 Oyama 2003, pp. 140–143.

The second letter reads:

> With regard to the present Higo Uprising and your prompt action in setting off to war, I thank you Kobayakawa Takakage and all the others who received commands concerning the punitive expedition against Wani and Hebaru, for your boundless loyalty; strictly investigate the remnants of the Higo *kunishū*, and on the 20th day of the 1st month of next year I will send envoys with over 20,000 men...[30]

The reference to sending in a team referred to as 'envoys' indicates that the overall situation in Higo still had to be brought under control with no repeat of the Sassa Narimasa fiasco. Both aims would be eventually realised, but it would take much longer than Hideyoshi could possibly have anticipated.

---

30 Oyama 2003, pp. 139–140.

9

The Harrying of Higo

Tanaka Castle may have fallen, but the Higo Rebellion still had six months to run as one by one the rebels whose names were introduced in an earlier chapter succumbed to Hideyoshi's forces. The process can be divided into three stages. First came the surrender of the castles close to Tanaka which were dealt with as part of the ongoing Tanaka campaign. Second were the more outlying seats of rebellion, while the final settlement, which took until early 1590 to achieve, involved securing political and military control of Higo by Sassa Narimasa's successors.

The first place to capitulate after Tanaka was Jōmura Castle. It had held out as long as Tanaka had survived, but when Tanaka fell Jōmura followed suit within 10 days. A ceasefire was proposed on 12m 15d (13 January 1588) and two days later Kobayakawa Takakage was able to report to Hideyoshi that it had surrendered.[1] The father and son team of Kumabe Chikanaga and Chikayasu, who had been the first rebels against Sassa Narimasa and had defended Jōmura so valiantly, were taken alive along with other family members. Chikanaga was placed in the custody of Tachibana Muneshige at Yanagawa Castle along with another of his sons, while Chikayasu was sent to Kokura. Accounts differ as to what happened to them. Chikayasu appears to have been executed at Kokura Castle along with several members of the loyal Yūdō family. Chikanaga would be killed a few months later on the orders of Hideyoshi's new representatives in Higo.[2]

The Kumabe family's resistance continued for some time at Shimono Castle in Ueki District in the person of another son of Kumabe Chikanaga who had been adopted into the Uchikoga family. It will be recalled that the Uchikoga had been responsible for one of the first victories over Narimasa's army when they ambushed and killed his nephew Sassa Muneyoshi on his way to Kumamoto. Uchikoga Shigefusa and Uchikoga Shigeteru then combined their forces at Shimono Castle and defied Hideyoshi in solidarity with Tanaka and Jōmura. Shimono was a strong place and had withstood a 3,000-strong Shimazu army in 1581, so Sassa Narimasa wisely left it alone until Tanaka was pacified and only launched a serious attack on 12m 13d

---

1   Araki 2012, p. 84.
2   Araki 2012, pp. 98–99.

(11 January 1588). After being driven back by fierce fighting involving much exchange of gunfire Narimasa's general set up siege lines. It was an expression of his confidence in gaining an ultimate victory, if nothing else. The news of the surrender of Jōmura concentrated many minds within the Shimono garrison, so their commanders decided to break out of the castle under the cover of heavy rain and make an escape, which they did on 12m 27d (25 January). Uchikoga Shigefusa sought refuge in Makino Castle, while Shigeteru headed further afield to the protection of the Shōdai family to await further developments.[3]

The fate of the Uchikoga, along with all the other surviving rebels, would ultimately be decided by the new force Hideyoshi ordered to the province on 1m 20d (16 February 1588). This formidable contingent consisted of the persons and armies of the Jōshi-shū: Hideyoshi's seven representatives (literally the shogun's envoys) whose names will be familiar to anyone who has studied Hideyoshi's campaigns. In overall command of the 20,000-strong force was Hideyoshi's brother-in-law Asano Nagamasa (1546–1611) who entered Kumamoto Castle in order to supervise the operation. Serving under him were Hachisuka Iemasa (1558–1639), Toda Katsutaka (?–1594), Ikoma Chikanori (1526–1603), Fukushima Masanori (1561–1624) and Konishi Yukinaga (1558–1600). The final member of the Jōshi-shū was the famous Katō Kiyomasa (1562–1611), whose name was to be indelibly associated with Higo Province for many years to come.

Most of the generals who had fought during the Tanaka campaign now returned home. The notable exception was Tachibana Muneshige, who owned the former Wani family possessions. He was still highly involved with the Higo Rebellion, and his name and that of Ankokuji Ekei crop up time and again in the purges that followed. Theirs and the Jōshi-shū's role was twofold: to complete the pacification of the province by seeking out and destroying all remaining centres of opposition, and to carry out a rapid yet thorough land survey so that Higo might be governed

The most influential figure to become involved with Higo Province after the rebellion was Katō Kiyomasa (1562–1611). He inherited the former sites of revolt and crushed all the remaining opposition with great ruthlessness. This statue of him in his characteristic tall helmet stands in front of Kumamoto Castle, which Kiyomasa built in 1611.

---

3   Araki 2012, pp. 68–71.

properly after they had left. The survey would be concluded after three months work and assessed Higo's productive capacity as 540,000 *koku*.[4] The pacification programme took much longer to complete and was carried out with considerable ruthlessness, although in several cases mercy was shown to infants who were then adopted into other families and grew to adulthood to serve local *daimyō*.

The first surviving rebel that the Jōshi-shū had to deal with was Uchikoga Shigefusa. He had defied Narimasa's army at Shimono and had also been responsible for the death of Sassa Muneyoshi, but even that record does not seem to have dissuaded him from the possibility of making a deal with his conquerors in the time-honoured manner of an *ukimusha*. On hearing that Hideyoshi's representatives were now in Higo, Shigefusa chose to leave the security of Makino Castle and journeyed confidently to Yanagawa Castle in order to plead his case with Tachibana Muneshige and Ankokuji Ekei. His hosts sought advice from the Jōshi-shū, who ordered that Shigefusa should be placed under house arrest and disposed of in some way, so Ekei and Muneshige decided to invite Shigefusa to the annual peach blossom festival on 3m 3d (29 March). The naive Shigefusa accepted, but his close retainers feared a trap, so on their advice Shigefusa feigned illness and declined the invitation. Shigefusa soon became resigned to the fact that his enemies planned to kill him anyway, so he resolved to go gloriously to his end, and on the morning of the festival day he led a dawn raid on Yanagawa Castle at the head of 250 men. They were stopped at the Kuromon, the castle's 'black gate' by a hail of musket fire. Driven back, Shigefusa committed suicide. His head was secured without disgrace by one of his retainers who took it back to the family temple. Shigefusa's mother and favourite concubine had been with him at his lodgings, and when the Tachibana force attacked it in turn his concubine dressed herself in Shigefusa's armour robe. Together with his mother they seized their *naginata* and while reciting the *nembutsu* prayer cut their way into the enemies until both were killed.[5]

Among other prominent names to feel the impact of the new force in Higo was its archetypal floating warrior Ōtsuyama Iekado. On 4m 8d (23 April) representatives were sent to Kamio Castle, ostensibly to engage in peace talks with him at a nearby temple, but one of the negotiators was more than he appeared. After gaining the confidence of Iekado he engaged him in a drinking bout and seized the moment to slice off his head.[6] On learning that Iekado was dead his younger brother Ienao attacked the nearest Sassa army but was repulsed and forced to flee by boat to Hizen Province, where he eventually died of illness.[7] All that was left of the family was the three-year-old son of Iekado. He was spared and went to Yanagawa, where he eventually entered the service of the Tachibana under the name of Seki Sukenao.

The formerly loyal Nawa family of Uto Castle also suffered in the purge. When Hideyoshi had invaded Kyushu Nawa Akitaka submitted to him, was

---

4   Araki 2012, p. 91.
5   Araki 2012, pp. 94–96.
6   Araki 2012, pp. 96–97.
7   Oyama 2003, p. 152.

reconfirmed in his landownings, and became one of the few barons who did not rebel against Sassa Narimasa. Akitaka, however, fell foul of the clause in Hideyoshi's letter of 12m 27d requiring the Jōshi-shū to seek out and punish any who 'who did not serve with loyalty in the present war, those who did not set out to war and those who sat on the fence'. Akitaka had tried to stay neutral, so he was summoned to Osaka to give an account of his inaction. He left his younger brother Akiteru in charge of Uto, who received the hostile attentions of the Jōshi-shū simply because his castle was needed in their plans for the resettlement of Higo. Akiteru refused to hand it over, and when military pressure was brought to bear upon him he requested help from the Shimazu of Satsuma: a most unwise choice. When he attempted to flee in that direction the Shimazu followed instructions from the Jōshi-shū and killed Akiteru on 4m 16d (1 May). His father Akitaka never returned to Higo. Instead, just like the heir of the Ōtsuyama, he became a loyal retainer of the Tachibana and ended his days in 1594 from wounds sustained while serving Hideyoshi in the invasion of Korea.

The reason why Uto Castle had to be confiscated was that it was one of three strongholds in Higo Province that the Jōshi-shū had decided were to be the bases for its future governance. Hideyoshi had concluded that one of the lessons of the Sassa disaster was that Higo was too large for one man to rule, so it was to be divided into three parts. The district of Kuma was to be retained by the great survivor Sagara Yorifusa and was assessed at 22,000 *koku,* while the rest of the province was divided between Katō Kiyomasa and Konishi Yukinaga. Yukinaga, one of the most celebrated of Japan's *kirishitan daimyō,* was given four districts of central Higo: Uto, Mashiki, Yatsushiro and the Amakusa Islands, with a total value of about 200,000 *koku.* Katō Kiyomasa received nine districts that totalled 194,500 *koku,* one of which was Ashikita in central Higo. The other eight: Tamana, Aso, Yamaga, Yamamoto, Kikuchi, Kōshi, Akita and Takuma, were the most northerly districts in the province and had been the sites of the Higo Rebellion.

On 6m 27d (19 August) each went to his chosen headquarters. Konishi Yukinaga took over Uto Castle. Katō Kiyomasa was given Kumamoto Castle, from where he was to play a decisive role in ending the Higo Rebellion, and few places in Japan are so firmly associated with one man as Kumamoto is with Katō Kiyomasa. In time he would replace the existing fortress by the magnificent palace castle seen today, and his bewhiskered face under a tall helmet still dominates the city, from dramatic bronze statues to souvenir dolls.

Because he had inherited the former centres of revolt Kiyomasa immediately began to disarm and even liquidate anyone whose loyalty was still suspect. Imprisonments and executions followed with the same ruthless efficiency that he had already demonstrated while he was still only one member of the Jōshi-shū. His victims then were the family of Shimonojō Tsunetaka, the keeper of Shimonojō Castle in the remote northeast of Higo beyond Mount Aso. He had joined the Higo Rebellion because of his obligations towards the Kumabe family, but his near neighbours stayed loyal to Sassa Narimasa throughout the campaign. One of them, Kitazato Masayoshi, was ordered to destroy Shimonojō, although Hideyoshi also commanded Ōtomo

Yoshimune to cross the border from Bungo and do the deed.[8] Yoshimune does not appear to have been needed, because the Kitazato completed the task on their own, and as a reward they received the Shimonojō territories. It is at this point that Katō Kiyomasa enters the story, because on the intercalary 5m 14d (7 July 1588) he sent an order to the Kitazato stating, 'Even though Shimonojō Sakon is slain, his wife and children are hiding somewhere and must be found and killed'. The Kitazato carried out the request, as would be confirmed in a letter from Kiyomasa on 6m 7d (30 July 1588), which reads as follows: 'Shimonojō Iga was planning to hide at Hita in Bungo but was killed; his head and those of four of his followers have been despatched and verified'.[9]

The search and destroy operation lasted until November 1588. In separate operations Kiyomasa sought out the son of the chief vassal of Kumabe Chikanaga, who had been killed at Waifu Castle, and also put to death Taku Munesada, who had betrayed Waifu to Narimasa. Treachery, clearly, was not enough to endear oneself to Katō Kiyomasa.[10] Later victims included Usumano Munesato, who died heroically with his ancestor's sword in hand, but in his fury he struck the lintel of the ceiling and the sword broke, at which point he was cut down.[11] In one of the last purges of all Higo Province acquired another dead samurai whose deified spirit would be associated with healing. This was Kai Sōryū, who had been forced to withdraw from the attack on Kumamoto castle after being severely wounded in his arms and legs. Accounts vary as to whether he died during the retreat or later at the hands of Katō Kiyomasa, but he is deified at the Kai Shrine in the Kashima District of Kumamoto as Ashite Kōjin, the *kami* of the limbs, and offerings are made to his spirit for help with diseases of the arms and legs.[12]

Shimonojō Tsunetaka, the keeper of Shimonojō Castle in Oguni District, was one of the last of the Higo rebels to capitulate. The site of his castle's honmaru is indicated by the two tall trees high above the spectacular waterfall.

8   Oyama 2003, pp. 146–147.
9   Araki 2012, pp. 100–101.
10 Araki 1987, p. 134; Oyama 2003, p. 155.
11 Miyao 2000, p. 28; Oyama 2003, p. 156.
12 Araki 2012, pp. 89–90.

At the Kai Shrine in Kumamoto the kokujin Kai Sōryū has become Ashite Kōjin, the kami of the limbs. Sōryū was forced to withdraw from the siege of Kumamoto Castle after being severely wounded in the arms and legs, hence the association.

The last of the Higo rebels to be overcome was Uchikoga Shigeteru, who had fled from Shimono Castle along with his adopted elder brother Shigefusa, and his fate illustrates the power that the Jōshi-shū now had over the floating barons of Higo. Shigeteru had sought sanctuary with the Shōdai family, who had not been part of the rebellion, but instead they forced him to return to Makino Castle. Tachibana and Ankokuji then roused the local *kokujin* against Shigeteru, branding him a traitor to the new situation of peace, and one of their number attacked Makino on 9m 20d (8 November). Shigeteru entrusted his six-year-old brother to a retainer so that the family line could be continued. He then set fire to Makino and died in the flames along with 14 surviving followers. The boy was spirited away to a secluded temple and lived to adulthood to serve the Kuroda under the name of Hattori Shigenao. Just like the last of the Ōtsuyama, the Nawa and all the other floating warriors who had been spared destruction, he caused no trouble to Hideyoshi for the rest of his life.[13]

13   Araki 2012, pp. 102–103; Oyama 2003, pp. 150–151.

The Death of Sassa Narimasa

And what of the man whose mismanagement had brought about the crisis? The revolt against Sassa Narimasa had been quelled successfully, but Narimasa was left with little personal credit to his name. Contrary to the once accepted view of him leading the attack on Tanaka, Narimasa seems to have left Kumamoto for Yatsushiro during the operation and stayed there during the latter stages of the siege at least, where he had ample opportunity to reflect upon his failure. The Higo Rebellion had been a revolt that he himself had brought about by bad management, and the ending of it had required a massive waste of resources, much time and the deaths of two close family members. Yet Sassa Narimasa was defiant to the last and did not take his failure lying down. No doubt expecting that Hideyoshi would punish him, he appealed for support among his peers.

This is the grave of Sassa Narimasa in the Hōonji temple in Amagasaki, the site of his act of suicide.

Unfortunately for Narimasa, his lost cause also attracted the attention of the Shimazu. Seeking to take advantage of the chaos in Higo Shimazu Yoshihiro began moving into the province from Satsuma on 2m 5d (13 March 1588), ostensibly to aid Narimasa in his continuing troubles with the revolt. A renewed threat from the Shimazu could not be tolerated, so Sagara Yorifusa blocked his progress at the border and fortified Sashiki Castle.[14] Hideyoshi was furious, both at the astonishingly defiant Shimazu and the hapless Sassa Narimasa. Not long after this highly embarrassing development Narimasa was summoned to Osaka by Hideyoshi to give an account of himself, but on 4m 3d (18 April 1588) he was arrested and detained at the Hōonji temple in Amagasaki without ever meeting his master. Two months later he was ordered to commit suicide, an act which he performed in some style at the Hōonji on the intercalary 5m 14d (7 July 1588).[15] His death is described as follows:

---

14 Araki 2012, pp. 144 & 204; Oyama 2003 p. 155.
15 Araki 2012, pp. 104–105.

Sassa Kuranosuke went out into the garden and sat down on a stone. Calling his equerry, he gave him thirty gold pieces and told him that he could have his wardrobe also, directing him. to advertise the fact that this stone was the one on which Kuranosuke sat for the last scene of his life. Then he cut open his belly in the form of a cross and tore out his guts. 'Now is the time!' he exclaimed when this was done to his satisfaction, and stretched out his neck, whereupon Todo Izumi, who was acting as his second, struck off his head.[16]

Epilogue on Amakusa

Having quelled almost all surviving opposition by the end of August 1588, Higo's two new *daimyō* were greatly helped in their new goal of preventing such outrages from breaking out again by the proclamation on 8m 8d (28 September 1588) of Hideyoshi's Sword Hunt, whereby any recalcitrant local militias, temples and villagers were forcibly disarmed.[17]This was the operation by which Hideyoshi's agents confiscated all weapons from anyone except a *daimyō*'s followers, most of whom were slowly being removed from the land, assigned to castles and placed in a state of vassalage to Hideyoshi's appointees chosen from his most loyal generals.[18] As noted earlier, the Sword Hunt was one reform in a package of three that would change Japan forever. The nationwide land survey was already under way, and rapid progress was being made towards the total separation of the warrior and farmer classes. In practice the urbanisation element of the separation process took much longer to take effect than the loss of cultivator status, so for many years there would be two types of samurai within a typical *daimyō* organisation. Some still received their incomes from lands while others were already fully stipendiary, and nowhere was the partial nature of the change better illustrated than in the extraordinary series of events that happened on the Amakusa Islands, which saw a brief re-run of the Higo Rebellion.

Up to that point the *kokujin* of Amakusa, isolated in their offshore territories, had remained aloof from the tumultuous events happening on the mainland. Their five baronial families had not defied Sassa Narimasa, but neither had they supported him, and their self-confidence was boosted in 1588 when Konishi Yukinaga was made their overlord because they shared his allegiance to Christianity. In reality it was probably the only positive thing the independent-minded barons could find in his favour, but it certainly provided a welcome contrast to the animosity towards Christian belief that was displayed by Katō Kiyomasa.

For some time the *kirishitan kokujin* of Amakusa enjoyed the anachronistic paternalism that had once characterised all of Higo. The incident that sparked the confrontation began on 8m 1d (10 September 1589) when Yukinaga ordered them to supply corvée labour for the building of Uto Castle. Amakusa Hisatane and Shiki Rinsen refused to comply, arguing that

---

16 Sadler 1937, p. 135.
17 Araki 2012, pp. 108–111.
18 Fujiki 2005, p. 59.

whereas they would be willing to undertake public works under Hideyoshi's direct control, the construction of Uto Castle was a private enterprise by a neighbour who did not actually rule them and to whom they were under no obligation. If Konishi Yukinaga needed a pretext for asserting his authority over the islanders he now had one, so on 9m 22d (31 October) he despatched a general called Ijichi Bundayū with 3,000 troops to march against Rinsen.[19] The Ijichi force advanced without hindrance, unaware that they were being led into a trap, and on 9m 25d (3 November) Juan Shiki Rinsen caught and massacred them.[20] This changed the dispute from an act of defiance into an armed rebellion, so Hideyoshi ordered Katō Kiyomasa to assist Yukinaga in bringing the Amakusa Islands under control.

Shiki Rinsen's Christian connections had provided him with a bonus in the form of Portuguese cannons, which he used to put up a spirited defence of Shiki Castle that lasted eight days from the initial armed contact being made on 11m 3d (10 December).[21] The focus of the Amakusa Rebellion then shifted to Hondo Castle, where a siege began that rivalled Tanaka in its tenacity if not its longevity. It was led by Katō Kiyomasa, and letters from the Jesuit missionaries then active in Japan contrast the savagery he displayed with the Christian devotion shown by the defenders, noting how, before going into battle, they made their confessions to the priests as stray bullets whizzed past their heads. The more sympathetic Konishi Yukinaga appears to have taken no part in the fighting until he was requested by Katō Kiyomasa to attack the back gate. He then delayed his assault so as to give the Christian defenders time to escape or may even have arranged an evacuation. Hondo surrendered later that same day of 11m 25d (1 January 1590).

The siege of Hondo Castle was the last major act of defiance against Hideyoshi within Higo Province, but one final pathetic scene was left to be played. Throughout the time of conflict the two Aso brothers whose sacred lineage had dissuaded certain kokujin from rebelling had been held hostage in Kumamoto. In 1588 Katō and Konishi split them up so that the younger one became a prisoner in Uto, but in 1592 a strange incident occurred. This was the Umekita Rebellion: a brief mutiny among the retainers of the Shimazu as they were preparing to leave for the Korean invasion. The leader was a certain Umekita Kunikane, whose insurrection involved a token invasion of Higo and the occupation of Sashiki Castle. The revolt was rapidly crushed, but a retainer of the Sagara who bore a grudge against the Aso family made the wild allegation that the child priest Aso Koreteru was its true ringleader. Hideyoshi believed him, and the pathetic creature was required to commit suicide in 1593. Thus did an 11-year-old boy become the final victim of the resistance to Hideyoshi in Higo Province, a long series of rebellions that ended not with a bang, but with a whimper.[22]

---

19 Tsuruta, Sōzō, 'Tenshō Amakusa Kassen no kōsatsu', *Kumamoto Shigaku* 55, 56 (1981), pp. 49–50.
20 Araki 1987:138.
21 Tsuruta 1981, p. 50; Araki 1987:139.
22 Asakawa 1929, pp. 333 & 393; Araki 1987, p. 136.

10

The Legacy of Tanaka

When Katō Kiyomasa became the *daimyō* of northern Higo the former Wani domain was among the lands he acquired, but Tanaka Castle was no longer needed and within a very short space of time it had virtually disappeared. The fire started by Hebaru Chikayuki had already taken all the castle superstructure with it, and in time the ditches became overgrown as the hill returned to its natural state to become virtually indistinguishable from the wooded slopes around. Acts of destruction by the besiegers had already wiped every trace of the Wani family from the valley. The burning of the Tōshōji destroyed almost every physical record of their existence, and even their ancestors' graves were deliberately obliterated by the victors.

In military terms the defence of the little castle of Tanaka had achieved something quite remarkable. A wooden fort on top of a small lump of volcanic rock had defied the mighty Toyotomi Hideyoshi for 100 days, and even though the outcome of the Higo Rebellion may never have been in any doubt Tanaka had shown how desperately a small position could be defended and how many resources would be needed to overcome it. During the 1990 symposium on Tanaka local historian Kunitake Yoshiteru proudly compared Tanaka's experience to that of the similar-sized Yamanaka Castle, which was stormed by Hideyoshi as part of the 1590 Odawara campaign. Tanaka defied Hideyoshi's army for one month; the *yamashiro* of Yamanaka lasted only one night.[1] His pride was shared by the other speakers, one of whom referred to Tanaka as 'a castle unique in Japan'.[2]

The significance of the siege of Tanaka lies not in the exercise of any great direct influence on historical events. Its legacy is instead to be found in its position on the cusp of the change from Medieval to Early Modern Japan, a political, social and military transformation that Tanaka exemplifies and encapsulates better than any other contemporary campaign. As the perfect exercise in micro-history, the whole sweep of Sengoku Japan is contained within the snapshot of history that Tanaka provides. In addition to marking this transition, the significance of rebellions like Tanaka, even if most of them were quickly suppressed, lies in the fact that they disprove two popular

---

1   Kunitake 1993, p. 138.
2   Kunitake 1993, p. 139.

A fragment of iron armour excavated from Tanaka Castle. It is probably a section of a kusazuri (armour skirt) that hung from the waist of the dō (body section).

notions. The first is that Hideyoshi's military campaigns were conducted only against very big fish; the second is that once a *sengoku daimyō* capitulated the rest of the territory's inhabitants fell meekly into line. Tanaka shows that *kokujin* had minds of their own.

Tanaka's other contribution to Japanese history lies in the valuable information it provides about Sengoku Period warfare. Later and richer castles would have their excavated mounds clad in stone to produce the magnificent edifices that we see today, but Tanaka illustrates better than almost anywhere else the final flowering of the pre-stone mountain castle model and its experience of a siege. Firstly, the excavated castle site is a classic example of a small *yamashiro* and furnishes an immense amount of detail not found anywhere else, all of which can be precisely identified in the absence of the urban sprawl that has overtaken so many of Japan's historical sites. The excavations and the map also show the care and detail that went into enhancing a *yamashiro*'s defences in times of war. Secondly, Tanaka's unique battle map provides an unparalleled snapshot of a siege in progress, and because of the map the two heroic chronicles can be shown to have been based on fact. Above all Japan's oldest battle map freezes in time the moment before four military units surged forward to bring about the conclusion of Japan's greatest unknown samurai battle.

Tanaka, however, also calls into question the traditional understanding of Japan's greatest military myth: the meaning of the word samurai. The chronicles may reveal a nostalgia for a time of heroic single combat between the aristocratic individual samurai of ancestral legend, but it is firepower that drives the attackers away, and only a small minority of the defenders are samurai in anything like the conventional use of the term. Instead the *jizamurai* and their floating medieval barons were betrayed into the hands of a new force of warriors who were separated from the land and paid a stipend to fight for the lords to whom they had submitted. These new standing armies were samurai and nothing else, and within a year of the fall of Tanaka the Sword Hunt would demonstrate what a contrast they provided to the model that had preceded them. Before the Sword Hunt anyone in Sengoku Japan with anything to defend had to be an armed warrior of some sort. After that date – according to theory at any rate – the only armed warriors in existence were the members of the newly redefined samurai class, although subsequent events would show that the disarming of non-samurai had been far from complete. In 1638 38,000 armed rebels sprang up as from nowhere during the Shimabara Rebellion that took over a year to quell. Yet even though that revolt shook the confidence of the Tokugawa, it would ultimately be no more than an insult to the pride of the all-powerful samurai élite of the Edo Period.

Tanaka and Personal Memory

For almost four hundred years the story of the siege of Tanaka Castle lived on beyond its immediate environments only as a footnote to the great events of Hideyoshi's reign. By way of contrast, within a short distance from the castle its memory was kept very much alive by the local people who tended the graves of the deified victims. The shrine to Wani Gozen enshrined the bringer of rain, while three particular graves were cared for with no evidence of bias towards friend or enmity towards foe. So not far from Tanaka Castle may be found the grave of an ally: the 'floating warrior' Ōtsuyama Iekado; the grave of an enemy: the deaf samurai Yufu Ōinosuke; and the grave of a traitor: Hebaru Chikayuki.

For many centuries too there has been a personal family connection between certain local individuals and the senior retainers of the Wani family who are buried in the valley, although the most remarkable of these links is to be found in the graveyard of the Ono family at the Enichiji in Omuta. The descendants of Ono Shigeyuki, whose father had adopted Wani Munezane, are buried there. Munezane in turn adopted the late Chikazane's newborn

The Wani blood line was preserved because Wani Chikazane's brother and son were both adopted into the Ono family. The Ono family graves lie in the Enichiji, where a notice board (shown here as an insert) commemorates the family's famous twentieth century descendant: Yoko Ono, depicted with her husband John Lennon. At the time this picture was taken some of the Ono gravestones had been toppled by the 2016 Kumamoto earthquake.

son when the child's mother escaped from the burning castle. Through him the Wani bloodline continued within the Ono family, a lineage that achieved unexpected prominence during the twentieth century when a descendant of theirs called Yoko Ono married John Lennon.

Tanaka's final level of significance may be found in the way it encapsulates the image of the samurai in a modern Japan that has had to come to terms with an often violent past. On the second Sunday of every February local High School students honour the defenders' memory by providing foot soldiers for the annual battle reenactment. Perhaps not surprisingly, the lively event is not held at the castle itself but in the somewhat mundane environment of the car park of Nagomi Town Hall. Nevertheless, the use of blank-firing muskets, smoke and mounted samurai make for an entertaining hour, even if the historical details tend to get lost along the way. At Tanaka the sensitive subject of Japanese militarism has been safely located in a historic era where it can be neutralised peacefully, analysed academically and celebrated joyously.

On the second Sunday of February a lively and highly inaccurate re-enactment of the battle of Tanaka takes place in the car park of Nagomi Town Branch Office. Here a footsoldier swings his sword at a samurai as the smoke clears after the musket fire.

Appendix I

Wani Gundan (The Wani War Tale)

The Battle of Tanaka Castle

Wani Kageyu Chikazane was the lord of Tanaka Castle in the village of Wani in the district of Tamana. His father was called Jiyū and had one daughter and three sons. The daughter, the oldest child to be born to his wife, was married to Hebaru Noto-no-Kami Chikayuki, lord of Sakamoto Castle in Jichō. The second, a son, was Kageyu Chikazane. The third son was called Danjō. His height was seven *shaku* eight *sun,* and as for his strength he was powerful enough to pick up a three-legged iron cauldron.[1] The fourth son was called Jinki. His countenance was scarlet and his eyes gleamed; from infancy he was said to have been prone to hairiness all over and the strength in his hands and feet also made him more like a bear than a man. For this reason: that Jinki was a man but had the appearance of a devil, his father Jiyū habitually called him Jin-ki (man-devil); the old reading of his given name was the same: Jinki. Among their retainers were Ishihara Gyōbu, Haruno Tōya, Kusano Hayato, Matsuo Hyūga and Nakamura Jibushōyū, each of the five a hero who was a match for any thousand men. Chikazane and his brave men owned lands in the following neighbouring areas: in Tamana District the villages of Wani, Kichiji and Jichō, Imō in Yamaga District, Shiragi in Chikugo Province etc., over 120 *chō* in all.

It so happened that when, during the fourth month of the fifteenth year of Tenshō, Lord Toyotomi Hideyoshi left the capital for the chastisement of the Shimazu, Kageyu Chikazane journeyed to Kitanoseki[2] to meet him. After this he joined the vanguard and headed for Satsuma where he performed meritorious military service and was confirmed in his landholdings as a result of it. When the lord of Higo province Sassa Narimasa attacked Kumabe Jibudayū Chikanaga, lord of Yamaga Castle,[3] he received intelligence that the

---

1   The expression 'could pick up a tripod' is a Chinese one used for the legendary hero Yamato Takeru in *Kojiki* and *Nihongi*.
2   i.e. Nankan.
3   i.e. Jōmura.

Higo *kunishūikki* were attacking Kumamoto Castle. At this Narimasa built *tsukejiro* in two places to the east and west of Yamaga castle and left some of his retainers to defend them. Narimasa then returned to Kumamoto in person and organised its defences, but he heard that the men defending the *tsukejiro* in Yamaga were suffering from hunger because of a shortage of supplies. Because both of the forces under his command anticipated that supplies would be on their way, he despatched his retainer Tsuda Yohei to the mansion of Tachibana Muneshige, and entreated him to take charge of relieving the men of the *tsukejiro*. Muneshige consented and in response advanced in force into Higo province and entered the Yamaga *tsukejiro* with supplies.

At precisely that moment a messenger sent from Ōtsuyama Iekado arrived at the mansion of Chikazane to say that he had heard of Narimasa's request, and that he was sending supplies from the Chikugo area to the *tsukejiro* at Yamaga. 'If you agree, let us cooperate with Kumabe to block the road and drive away the Chikugo army', he suggested. Chikazane was in agreement and despatched Nakamura Jibu with over 100 men. Another 100 men from Ōtsuyama Iekado under the command of Nakamura Dewa and Morisuke from the same family assembled at the same place. When he got to hear of this, Hebaru Chikayuki also sent one hundred men as reinforcements. When they had combined their 300-strong army set out for the Hirano-Tateo area, where they heard that the Tachibana force had already taken the supplies into Yamaga.

A helmet designed in the shape of a human head, with a traditional samurai hairstyle realised using horse hair. This fine example is in Kawagoe Historical Museum.

As a consequence they waited to attack the Chikugo force on their way back, and this happened on the 7th day of the 9th month. Tachibana Muneshige had satisfactorily delivered the supplies to the *tsukejiro*, but Kumabe's retainers followed their trail and soon closed in on them. When the Chikugo army were about to pass through the vicinity of Hirano the Higo armies that were lying in wait struck simultaneously. Muneshige was unperturbed and Yufu Kazusa-no-suke, Ono Izumi, Jūji Settsu and others followed his lead and cut their way into the midst of the *ikki* army, where even the guards suffered wounds or were killed, and the *ikki* army came to the realisation that they were facing defeat in battle. Over half their number were chased away or exterminated. Nakamura saw this happen and was the only man who stood his ground; five other men who had offered resistance were killed by Tachibana's retainer Ikebe Ryūemon. During the course of this battle even Muneshige sustained injuries and a large number of his guards were also killed. Narimasa heard of this and was highly indignant and said that he would detach a large army under his command to attack Hebaru, Wani and Ōtsuyama. Hebaru Chikayuki got to hear of it and was greatly alarmed. He therefore made ready over 300 troops and came to Wani and was there with Chikazane when they laid siege to Tanaka Castle.

The layout of the siege was that at the castle's main gate the Hiakeguchi, Wani Danjō, Matsuo Hyūga and others waited with 150 men, 30 muskets and 20 bows. At the north gate below Miyadake Wani Jinki and Matsuo Ichinokami, Hyūga's son, waited with 100 men, 20 muskets and 20 bows. At the Shinshiroguchi was Nakamura Jibushōyū with 150 men, 20 muskets and bows and 20 spears. In the *honmaru* Hebaru Noto-no-kami Chikayuki was waiting with 300 retainers, 100 muskets, 80 bows and 50 spears. In the *ni no maru* the general Wani Kageyu Chikazane and others waited with over 100 men, 20 muskets, 30 bows and 30 spears. The captain of the *ukimusha* Kusano Hayato and others had a mobile unit of over 100 men, 20 muskets, 30 bows and 30 spears who were standing by and kept watch to provide instant back-up the moment the enemy attacked.

On the twenty-eighth day of the tenth month Sassa Mutsu-no-Kami Narimasa's army of over 8,000 troops came bearing down upon the above place. Reinforcements from Tachibana Sakon Shōkan and Nabeshima Kaga-no-Kami then made their appearance. They set up positions at Babada, Kurisaki, Hazekawa, Kanashikihara, Miyatake, Shibatsuka, Sakaibara and Hiakeguchi. Ten thousand men were packed into these restricted locations. Because of their encirclement it gave the appearance that the tops of mountains and the valleys were full of men. A strategy group then went to observe the castle. The insignificant little castle with 1,000 men, a small number that indicated Chikazane's boldness in accepting a siege, were now confined within a perimeter at a distanceof five *chō*. Because the enemy believed it would be swallowed in one gulp they did not prepare any siege equipment but instead set off for an immediate assault to overcome it.

Among them was Narimasa's retainer, a man called Matsubara Gorōemon Naomoto. Naomoto advanced carrying a long-shafted spear, and so that his abilities might be displayed called out, 'I am a person called Matsubara Gorōemon, a retainer of Sassa Narimasa. Let anyone willing come out!' From inside the castle Haruno Tōya heard this, stuck out his chest beneath his lacquered breastplate and replied, 'These boastful words will be cut short when I run you through!' Without a moment's hesitation Gorōemon advanced to within one *chō* of the castle's single fence. Tōya indicated his acceptance of the challenge by grabbing hold of his cormorant-headed spear. When Gorōemon made as if to respond Tōya was encouraged. Neither was inferior to the other in his great strength as they came together at a gap in the single fence with shouts of 'Eiya, Eiya!' In the end their spear shafts bent and snapped in the middle, and both men ended up flat on the ground like two dogs separated after a fight.

With this the battle began, and the initial attack was launched by our vanguard making an advance. The enemy in the vicinity received arrows that were notched and loosed one after another from the castle. There were a number of dead and wounded so they faltered and were killed or fled and were then mercilessly chased away. Within a very short space of time our attack had killed one hundred men. They then drew back to the castle and it was found that among the allies there had been only four or five men wounded in a couple of places and not even one man had been killed, thus was it said.

Usono Kurōdo Kills Wani Chikazane and the Castle Falls

The following day, the twenty-ninth, found Sassa Narimasa engaged in reflection. With even this overwhelming force he had not been able to take a little castle by storm; the fortress had plentiful supplies and the troops under command there were all of one heart. However, he had heard it said that Hebaru Chikayuki was greedy and was also a man with a weak sense of loyalty. So he hatched a plot to trick Chikayuki and make him kill Chikazane. An arrow letter was consequently loosed into the castle. Chikayuki opened it and perused the message. It read, 'The objective in this present war is to destroy the Wani brothers. It is certainly not to punish you. If you kill Chikazane and they surrender I will authorise that your original landholdings will revert to your possession as your own territory.' Chikayuki was greatly pleased, and immediately drew up his reply, 'When I kill Chikazane I will light a beacon as a signal. Please attack at that very moment.' The plan nevertheless had certain difficulties. As might be expected it could have been brought to a halt by Chikayuki's brave warriors, men who feared nothing, but there was a man called Usono Kurōdo, a retainer of Chikazane. Usono Kurōdo was a man of eloquence and was also very brave, and although Chikazane appreciated his qualities, at this present battle he had not been made a general. For that reason Kurōdo bore him a grudge, so Chikayuki secretly sent for Kurōdo and made an earnest request of him. Kurōdo agreed with the details, and in the middle of the night of the sixth day of the twelfth month he sneaked into Chikazane's private quarters and killed him, cutting off his head, and then escaped into the enemy lines. Chikayuki sent the signal by means of a beacon and the attack was launched. At the same time Hebaru set fire to the *honmaru* and because of a strong wind the castle was in an instant reduced to dust and ashes.

Realising that an attack was taking place the two men Wani Danjō and Jinki considered the matter and gathered their troops together. Realising that their general Wani Chikazane had been killed and that the castle would therefore quickly fall, 30 or 40 men of the survivors made mutual preparations and finally galloped into the enemy lines where they fought mercilessly. When they returned their comrades realised that half had been killed, because there were only 17 men left under the command of Danjō, Jinki, Ishihara Gyōbu, Nakamura Jibushōyū, Matsuo Hyūga, Matsuo Ichinokami and Haruno Tōya.

The Death of Wani Danjō

Wani Jinki placed into the safe hands of Haruno Tōya the wife of his elder brother Chikazane and their five-year-old daughter, who left by the North Gate as the castle fell and fled to Miike. From now on there was no thought in his head except the prospect of death; he was joined by men who felt the same and they fought desperately. Just then Sassa Narimasa's *samurai-taishō*, a brave warrior of great strength called Tsuda Yohei, charged at Danjō, who received him on his sword-hand side and slashed him from the brow of his helmet to his saddle. Yohei was almost cut into two halves and fell to the ground. When they saw this Yufu Ōinosuke from the Tachibana and Ushijima Fujishichi from the Nabeshima spearheaded an attack as one body. One of Nakamura Jibushōyū's picked troops who was hidden from view loosed an arrow that pierced Yufu Ōinosuke's breastplate and went through as far as the middle of his back so that he fell from his horse. Fujishichi advanced and Matsuo Hyūga grappled with him furiously, so that both of them fell off the cliff of Iwa Jizō and were killed. Matsuo Ichinokami and Ishihara Gyōbu received many severe wounds but this did not restrict their spirited efforts, even though men around them were killed. Wani Jinki was surrounded by over 20 men, cut down the eight nearest to him and in spite of a hand wound drove off seven others, he then galloped off and slipped away into the mountains alone, but whether he survived or died is not known.

By now Wani Danjō was the only man left standing. He drew his 4 *shaku* 8 *sun* sword and made his way into the attackers who surrounded him, scything them down as if they were rice, flax, bamboo or reeds. For a brief moment it seemed that he would be killed, but fortunately for him many soldiers came running up from as far away as one or two *chō* and soon both men and horses were trampling each other underfoot. Danjō made up his mind as the army approached. He calmly prepared for suicide and ascended Miyatake inside the castle. Two soldiers from the Sassa side, Jimbō Gorō and Sugino Mataichi, mistakenly thought he was fleeing and set off after him up the hill. Danjō saw this, drew his sword and threw it away, then opened his great arms and waited. The two men drew near from the left and the right, at which he seized them in his bare hands and with the two men held under his armpits, having decided to die and take them with him to the world of the dead, he dived off Miyatake into the valley bottom and perished.

Haruno Tōya entrusted Chikazane's wife and daughter to the care of the priest Seichō at the Tōshōji, the Wani family temple in the village, for them to be sent on to a certain Ono who lived in Miike in Chikugo Province. Tōya then headed into the midst of the enemy and was killed. After this the priest Seichō escorted Chikazane's wife and daughter to the Ono family. At the time of the fall of the castle Chikazane's wife was three months pregnant and when the time came she gave birth to a boy. The boy was adopted into the Ono family and called Ono Sakuzaemon. It is said that he is still living in Yanagawa in the same province.

According to another account, at this time Wani Danjō's wife, a 13-year-old girl, left the castle as well and threw herself into the river at a place below the castle called the Wani Rock. Her body was carried by the current three *ri* downstream to the village of Uchida; and at the place where she sank below the water was a rock that is now also called the Wani Rock, and local custom relates various ghostly stories. Future generations enshrined her spirit, naming her as the goddess of water, and at that area she is called Wani Gozen. It is said that at times of drought the local people pray to her in an earnest attempt to make it rain.

According to another account the orders to restore Hebaru Chikayuki's landholdings were not carried out, and it was the opinion that when he returned he ought to be put to death, so he wandered from place to place and died somewhere from illness. His retainer Imō Settsu-no-Kami accompanied [Hebaru's] son Jirō (otherwise called Kumaichi) who was then nine years old. He lived in seclusion in the village of Kichiji; at length Jirō changed his name to Jirōzaemon and served lord Katō Kiyomasa with a stipend of 350 *koku,* but he was killed in a quarrel with a comrade and the family name immediately became extinct. Imō Settsu-no-Kami was by now a *rōnin* and lived in the village of Sotome. A person who lived until about the Meireki and Manji periods [1655–1661] called Hebaru Gorō was said to be the son of this Settsu-no-Kami (His previous name was Imō Heizaemon; he had one daughter who did not produce a son so the family name died out). Gorō's grandfather Hebaru Hitachi Nyūdō Yoshimichi had received a letter from Ōtomo Yoshimune as follows.

> As to the matter of Chikasada, I grant a parcel of land to Hebaru Hitachi in reward for his good deeds in the battle. The details will follow in another communication. It will be 50 *chō*.
>
> Hebaru Hitachi Nyūdō-dono
> Yoshimune (red-seal)

From looking at the above Chikasada was Hebaru Noto-no-Kami Chikayuki's father and Hitachi Nyūdō was Chikasada's family's chief retainer (*karō*). He had a stipend of 12 *chō* at Imō in Yamaga. He lived in Imō castle and was called Imō Settsu-no-Kami.

According to another account Usono Kurōdo was hated by everyone around because of the murder of his lord and it is said that he became a beggar and died of starvation by the roadside.

This is from a manuscript borrowed from the Noda family storeroom and copied on the 2nd day of the 5th summer month of the 7th year of Meiwa [1770], Elder Brother of the Metal, the Year of the Tiger.

This present copy was made on the 26th day of the intercalary month of the 5th year of Bunsei [1822].

Appendix II

Wani no jō rakujō no oboe (Recollections of the Fall of Wani Castle)

This document leaves my hands as miscellaneous notes; that notwithstanding, I trust it will prove of some benefit.

Item, during the fourteenth year of Tenshō, at the time when Waifu Chikanaga and Yūdō Ōsumi planned an insurrection and secluded themselves within Yamaga Castle, Lord Sassa Mutsu-no-Kami first had to deal with the Aso-shū at Kumamoto castle; so Lord Mutsu-no-Kami drove the above besieging unit of Aso away from Kumamoto castle and then made a grand entrance. As a result of this the two men Wani Kageyu Chikazane and Hebaru Noto-no-Kami Chikayuki left Kumamoto and secluded themselves inside Wani castle, while Ōtsuyama Sukefuyu[1] shut himself up in Kamio castle in Otakuro. It was then that Lord Tachibana Sakon took supplies to the units at Yamaga castle, at which Ōtsuyama Sukefuyu, Wani Chikazane and Hebaru Chikayuki set out with their forces and attacked him at Hirano. After this there were peace talks with Jō[mura] castle, and the ultimate result was that Waifu Chikayasu committed *seppuku* in Yanagawa castle, while Yūdō Ōsumi was taken by Lord Ikoma, a samurai lord from Shikoku, and was killed at Kokura in Buzen. When news of this unexpected act of killing reached Yūdō's son Magoichi he feared being attacked and was forced to move away, fleeing by boat to Nagasaki.

Thus it was that during the first ten days of the tenth month of the fifteenth year of Tenshō, Wani Chikazane and Hebaru Chikayuki shut themselves up in Wani Castle, at which Ankokuji, a samurai lord from Chūgoku, with Kikkawa and Kobayakawa under his command, together with Chikushi Kōzuke of the Kyushu-shū, Nabeshima of Hizen, Tachibana Sakon and Sassa Mutsu-no-Kami, seven generals in all, arrived with men from thirteen provinces and took up positions for an attack. They assembled their forces at these locations: Lord Ankokuji to the west of the castle at Babada; Lord Kikkawa to

---

1   A mistake for Iekado.

the north-north-west of the castle at Kurisaki; Lord Kobayakawa to the north of the castle at Kanashikihara; Lord Nabeshima to the east-south-east of the castle at Shibatsuka; Lord Tachibana to the south of the castle at Sakaibara opposite the castle's Hiakeguchi. Frequent clashes subsequently took place.

From within Lord Tachibana's unit Miyako Gorokubei went up to the castle fence holding his spear, and from within the castle a retainer of Chikazane's, a man called Haruno Tōya, took up his cormorant-headed spear and went through the fence; they introduced themselves, each announcing his name to the other, and the contest began; then Funo Shichi'emon a retainer of Lord Tachibana, galloped up and announced his name on arrival. Chikazane's retainer Nakamura Jibushōyū, a commander in the castle, went out and with his bow and arrow and loosed it at Shichiemon on his right side and made him fall. Many other honourable encounters also took place. As a result Ankokuji had to use his ingenuity to effect an entry. He decided that Chikayuki would be sympathetic, and that Chikazane's Usono Kurōdo would cut down Wani Chikazane and make an end of him. They would surrender when his head was displayed. So at early dawn of the fifth day of the last month of the year Chikayuki revealed his hand and sent his seven-year-old son and heir Kumaichi out of the castle to Ankokuji as a hostage, and at the Hour of the Snake he killed Chikazane. Thus did Chikayuki bring about the defeat, and pulled his attaching unit out to fight against Chikazane's retainers.

Chikazane's younger brother Wani Danjō drew his 4 *shaku* 8 *sun* long sword. He, his younger brother Wani Jinki and Chikazane's retainers Matsuo Hyūga and his son Ichinokami, shut themselves up within the Shinshiro. From out of the attacking unit of the lord of Hizen, Tsuda Yohei carried out repeated assaults; and the great force of Hizen caused many casualties. Wani Danjō, Jinki of the same family, Matsuo Hyūga and Ichinokami of the same family performed several meritorious deeds, until finally they were struck down and died. At dawn of the sixth day Chikayuki went down from the castle and was received by Nabeshima; he then went to Hizen.

As for Ōtsuyama Sukefuyu, on the 8th day of the 4th month of Tenshō 16 he was killed at the Jisho-In at Kichiji Village by two men called Uchika Nyūdenshichi and Shinnin Hōshi who were sent from lord Awa-no-Kami of Shikoku, and Iekado's younger brother Ienao went to Ōshima in Hizen Province. There he met his end, as is well recorded.

The First Year of Meireki [1656]; during the first ten days of the sixth lunar month
Nakamura Joshin Nyūdō
[Copied] on this day: the First Year of Shotoku [1711]; Junior Brother of the Metal, the Year of the Hare, First Day of the Eighth Month It is the property of the Kichiei family living in the village of Middle Wani in Tamana county in Higo Province.
[Copied] on this date: the Fifth Year of Bunsei [1822], Elder Brother of the Water, the Year of the Horse, Fifteenth Day of the Sixth Month.

Bibliography

The mon (badge) of a crane is traditionally associated with the Wani family of Tanaka, as shown on this banner.

Araki, Eishi, *Higo Kunishū Ikki* (Kumamoto: Shuppan Bunka Kaikan, 1987).

Araki, Eishi, *Higo Kunishū Ikki* (Kumamoto: Shuppan Bunka Kaikan, 2012).

Berry, Mary Elizabeth, *Hideyoshi* (Cambridge Mass: Harvard University Press, 1982).

Birt, Michael Patrick, *Warring States: A study of the Go-Hōjō daimyo and domain 1491–1590* (Ph.D Thesis, Princeton University, 1983).

Chamberlain, Basil Hall, 'A Short Memoir from the Seventeenth Century. "Mistress An's narrative"', *Transactions of the Asiatic Society of Japan* 15 (1887), pp. 37–40.

Elison, George and Smith, Bardwell, L. (eds.), *Warlords, Artists and Commoners: Japan in the Sixteenth Century* (Honolulu: University of Hawaii Press, 1981).

Elisonas, Jurgis, 'Christianity and the daimyo' In Hall, J.W. & McLain, J.L. (eds.), *The Cambridge History of Japan. Vol. 4 Early modern Japan* (Cambridge: Cambridge University Press, 1991), pp. 301–372.

Fujiki, H., *Katanagari* (Tokyo: Iwanami Shoten, 2005).

Gubbins, J.H. 'Hideyoshi and the Satsuma Clan in the Sixteenth Century' *Transactions of the Asiatic Society of Japan* (8, 1880), pp. 92–143.

Hale, J.R. 'The Early Development of the Bastion: An Italian Chronology *c*.1450–1534' in J.R. Hale (ed.) *Renaissance War Studies* (London: A.C. Black, 1983), pp. 1–29.

Hall, John Whitney, (ed.). *Japan Before Tokugawa: Political Consolidation and Economic Growth, 1500 to 1650* (Princeton: Princeton University Press, 1981).

Kumamoto City, *Kumamoto-shi shi kankei shiryōshū. Volume 4: Higo koki shūran* (Kumamoto: Kumamoto City, 2000).

Kunitake, Yoshiteru, *Tenshō Jidai to Wani ichizoku: Higo Kunishū Ikki* (Kumamoto: Kumamoto Kumamoto: Kumamoto Hibi Shimbun Jōhō Bunka Centre, 1993).

Kuroda, Yūji, 'Tanaka-jō ato hakkutsu chōsa gaiyō II' *Sengoku da yori* (5, 2005), pp. 5–6.

Miike Historical Society, *Ono-ke no keifu* (Miike Historical Society, Omuta, 2017).

Mikawa Town, *Tanaka-jō ato Volumes 11 & 12* (Tamana: Mikawa Town Board of Education, 1997).

Mikawa Town, *Katsuryoku to kosei aru chiiki zukuri (Toyotomi Hideyoshi gunzei to Tanaka-jō kōbōsen) Shinposium kanzen shūroku shū* (Tamana: Mikawa Town Board of Education, 1999).

Miyao, Yoichi (ed.), *Nankan Kibun* (Nankan City: Nankan Board of Education, 2010).

Nagabayashi, Shōin, *Hōsatsu gunki. Hisatsu gunkishū* (Tokyo: Rekishi Toshosha 1980).

Nagomi Town, *Wani Ishisan shiro ato* (Nagomi: Nagomi Board of Education, 2007).

Oyama, Ryūshu, *Hideyoshi to Higo Kunishū Ikki* (Fukuoka: Kaichōsha, 2003).

Sadler, A.L., *The Maker of Modern Japan: The Life of Tokugawa Ieyasu* (London: Allen and Unwin, 1937).

Sasama, Yoshihiko, *Buke senjin sahō shūsei* (Tokyo: Yūzankaku, 1968).

Sasama, Yoshihiko, *Zusetsu Nihon kassen bugu jiten* (Tokyo: Kashiwashobō, 2004).

Stavros, Matthew, 'Military Revolution in Early Modern Japan', *Japanese Studies* (33, 2013), pp. 243–261.

Tanaka, Hiroshi, 'Go-aisatsu' *Sengoku da yori* (4, 2004), p. 1.

Tsuruta, Sōzō, 'Tenshō Amakusa Kassen no kōsatsu' *Kumamoto Shigaku* 55,56 (1981), pp. 47–58.

Turnbull, Stephen, 'The ghosts of Amakusa: localised opposition to centralised control in Higo Province, 1589–90.' *Japan Forum* 25 (2, 2012), pp. 191–211.

Various Authors, *Nihon Jōhaku Taikei Vol. 18* (Tokyo: Shinjimbutsu, 1979).

Yoshida, Y. (ed.), *Taikō-ki* Volume II (Tokyo: Kyōikusha, 1979).